W9-CHV-057

The WebPowered Entrepreneur

The WebPowered Entrepreneur

A Step by Step Guide

Lisa Chapman

Dunham Books
Nashville, Tennessee

The WebPowered Entrepreneur

For information regarding special sales or licensing,
please contact the publisher:

Dunham Books
63 Music Square East
Nashville, Tennessee 37203

www.dunhamgroupinc.com

ISBN 978-0-9837-456-6-2
Printed in the United States of America

Dedication

I tip my hat to all who have gone before,
to those who have pioneered the digital universe and paved the way
for us to benefit from their hard-won triumphs.

Table of Contents

Introduction

As a career entrepreneur, and now a business and social media consultant as well (www.lisachapman.com), I passionately proclaim that these are exciting times for the entrepreneur. The exponential growth of the Internet provides powerful opportunities to attract new customers, increase sales and continue to grow. A strategically built website and social marketing plan work together to command traffic, profits, and long-term value.

Whether you already run a business, or you wish to start one, this book is invaluable to build your brand and increase your customer base.

If you already run a business, I recommend that you focus on the chapters that most interest you. However, going over the basics, such as choosing a hot niche or building a dynamic site, usually helps every reader. Undoubtedly, you'll pick up great tips or consider concepts that may have changed dramatically since you set yours up.

The WebPowered Entrepreneur is for anyone who says, *"Just show me how. I'll do it."* This is NOT a get-rich-quick guide. But if you recognize a great business opportunity, and are willing to put some thoughtful time and effort into it, you can successfully build your business online - and offline, too.

We'll discuss 'products', but I use it in the general sense, so the term actually means *both* products and services. The Internet is the perfect place to promote a service business, too.

People all over the globe are building their businesses and making money by marketing online - every single day. A great many others simply haven't done it yet because the Internet changes so fast. Unless you are online full-time - searching, learning, and keeping up with all things state-of-the-art—it's often overwhelming and confusing.

This book is my commitment to make the dream of using the Internet and social media marketing achievable for anyone who is willing and able to do it. The Internet has finally reached a point at which certain strategies, tools, and tactics are easy and reliable, and can be used together to grow profitable businesses. *You can do it, too.*

In *The WebPowered Entrepreneur*, you get just enough detailed, step-by-step, "How-To" instruction for making money on the Internet – and tap into the explosive power of social media. Social media is the vehicle that delivers your brand to the masses. Using social media, your business commands awareness, followers, connectors, promoters, and ultimately, customers and *revenue!*

The book details a nuts-and-bolts strategy that you can apply to any product or service. In these pages, I give you specific directions and examples with related links. I walk you through each phase of building your business and explain why it is important. Each step is like a building block. You are the builder and, within this system, you can customize the steps for your own business.

Social media is not a mystery. The following pages give you the lay of the land, with insights to how social media works in general and how it is used day to day.

Social media is the new digital marketing frontier and this book teaches you how to use it to achieve your business building goals. Social media does not have to be overwhelming. In fact, if you follow this method, it's much easier and quicker than traditional media. You don't need a Rolodex of professional PR contacts and years of media relationships.

With a few insider steps, you can achieve first page Google ranking within days.

I'll show you how.

Social media is much more than just setting up accounts on Facebook, Twitter, LinkedIn and YouTube. Effective use of social media takes deeper understanding, planning, and consistent execution. Social media that makes money is deliberately planned and executed.

It's relatively easy. The Internet is packed with well-developed platforms and online tools that make building your business efficient and lucrative. I cut to the chase for you - just enough detail to direct you, not so much that it's confusing.

It's affordable. You can build your business with online tools that don't cost much. In fact, many of them are free. In these pages, you get links, instruction, tips and more online resources. If a certain rabbit hole intrigues you, follow the links to learn more and customize to your heart's content.

You can do this part-time. Then, as you see results, keep building! The resources at the end of the book offer more in-depth information that can take you and your new business beyond the basics.

Social media is growing like crazy. And here's the great news: it's still in its *infancy*. You are actually entering the market *early!* So step up and take a swing. The playing field has been leveled, and even without experience, you can hit the ball out of the park.

Now *you* can finally be one of those fortunate individuals who make it happen. Enjoy the ride.

To find updates and helpful new tools that may not have been available at the time of publication, I publish a companion website for additional resources. A complete downloadable list of links is also available on the book's website:

http://www.TheWebPoweredEntrepreneur.com

I welcome comments, updates, suggestions, constructive criticism, reader reviews and endorsements. If you find broken links, please let me know! When you contact me, I may not be able to respond to all, depending upon the volume, but I WILL read them all. To email me: Feedback@TheWebPoweredEntrepreneur.com

In the book, I recommend tools that are either free or low cost. Many times, the paid tools offer additional functionality over the free tools, which I believe warrants the price – and many can be used free for a trial time period. When I recommend a paid tool, I also make every effort to identify alternative free tools that readers may also try.

I have used many of the tools and tactics contained herein, but have not used all of them. In such cases, I have researched them thoroughly (through independent user reviews and other detailed information, both from expert sources and information that is available publicly) to form my own opinion that they are quality, cost-effective tools - and are reasonable, worthwhile investments. This is my opinion only, and the reader should evaluate each tool for their own intended purpose.

One of the challenges of all authors and publishers that offer information related to the Internet is to help the reader stay up-to-date. Although every effort has been made to ensure the accuracy of the information offered in this book at the time of printing, errors and omissions may occur, or information may change subsequent to the date of publication. Internet sites, tools, and tactics change at the speed of light.

To find updates and helpful new tools that may not have been available at the time of publication, I publish a companion website for additional resources. A complete downloadable list of links is also available: http://www.TheWebPoweredEntrepreneur.com

About my professional services: I enjoy helping others establish and grow their businesses, both online and offline. For more information about my business and social media consulting services, see: www.LisaChapman.com for more tips, visit my Marketing and Social Media blog: http://www.managementhelp.org/blogs/marketing/

Chapter One

***

So You Want to Build Your Business Online?

Build a profitable online business *doing something you love!*

You want to sell something online and make a great income, right?

The beautiful thing is you *can* achieve online business success in the industry of your choice, doing something you love.

There are millions of pages on the Internet that claim to have the secret to riches. I've spent countless hours, over many years with my face buried in the computer screen, testing and evaluating these claims and their business models. Most of them offer only a small sliver of the information you need to build a profitable, sustainable business. And many of them are old, with outdated technology or incomplete offerings.

The Internet changes fast, and so do the "best practices" and social media capabilities for creating, marketing, and maintaining your online business. These pages pull together all the relevant, updated information that you need.

If you have a business, either offline or online, this book will give you the understanding and tools you need to either establish or expand your business online. It's critical to first understand how the Internet works so you can build your rock solid foundation. Internet tools may help you leverage your time, but if your business is not built to last, it probably won't. So whether you're an Internet business newbie, or an experienced business owner, take heed of the online fundamentals. Apply them to your business for the best chance of growth and profitability over the long-term.

What's the difference between online business success and failure? Most times, it comes down to just a few key things – things that weren't quite right or not complete. Had they been executed better, the business would have been profitable. The problem is that most people are willing and able, but just don't know what those few key success factors are. I offer my own top-level success factors to get you started thinking on the right path.

Success Factor 1:
Start with a proven, profitable method

If you're serious about building a solid business, the Internet is not the place for invention. Instead, follow the methods that have worked for others, and don't skip, scrimp or stall. Follow the steps, build carefully, and achieve the same results.

Even if you're building your online business part-time and you're squeezed for hours, it won't work if you gloss over the details. Online, details make all the difference in the world. Pay close attention to gain the advantage over the person who doesn't. And believe me – you will encounter many who don't. If that sounds too tedious for you, then think long and hard before undertaking this project. Details separate the good from the great – the profitable from the unprofitable. Make a commitment now to pay close attention to details and strive for excellence at each step.

Success Factor 2:
Choose a profitable niche

On the Internet, it's all about the niche. A niche is a subset of a broader market. A niche is narrowly defined, with customers that can be clearly targeted. For example, Artists may be considered a broad target market. More specifically, Musical Artists are a set within the broader category and the subset of Jazz Musicians are a niche. Jazz musicians could be even further divided into those who write their own music versus those who only perform others' songs.

Clearly define your target audience. It should be a segment that has pressing needs or problems to solve. Internet users search for information and products that help them make money, save money, solve a problem or meet a need. Sometimes that need is desire or hope. When your message promises to fulfill any of these, you will likely have a profitable online business.

Later, I show you how to clarify your ideal customer profile. Don't skip this step, as it is critical to your success. With this in mind, your niche is the central concept to develop your site, choose your products or services, craft your messages, create your promotional strategy, and drive customers to your site.

Success Factor 3:
Engage the right tools

The Internet is all about tools, and they're evolving at lightening speed.

Anytime you can automate a task with a recommended tool that's easily integrated into your system, use it! Tools are your ticket to leverage your time. They enable you to focus on the most important and most enjoyable tasks.

Online tools in general, and social media tools in particular, are becoming more sophisticated and automated. They allow you to leverage your time and your network. They enable you to grow your business more quickly than offline. Social media offers you the opportunity to spread your message virally – quickly! And that's the holy grail of Internet business. When you create a message and engage tools that spread your message throughout your chosen niche, chances are that you will be very, very successful.

Don't be *penny wise and pound foolish*. Granted, many online tools are free. But sometimes, those free versions don't do the full job. Perhaps they may serve you in the beginning, but the premium (paid) version of the tool would do the whole job and scale with your business. I advise you to make discerning choices. Use the free tools when you can, and when it doesn't cost you more time in the long run. But if a paid tool gives you an automated process that's more effective, then take that initial financial plunge and invest in the most efficient, effective tools that free you up to spend your time and talents doing what you do best – and grow your business to the next level. You intend success, so build a strong foundation for success.

Success Factor 4:
Promote online and build your list

As you will realize in the pages that follow, your long-term success rests solidly on the quality, size and effective use of your email list.

The steps in this book work successfully together to build your business on a solid foundation. *Effectively promoting your business online drives traffic and builds your email list, when you capture visitors' contact information through 'opt-ins' and 'autoresponders'* (we cover those later). Your email list – your sizable, highly targeted customer base – is the key to ongoing profits and longevity.

The entrepreneurs who make money online all have that in common. Not to minimize the rest of the things that you do to create and build your business, in the end, your email list is *your most important asset.*

What is "social media?" According to Wikipedia, "Social media is media designed to be disseminated through social interaction, created using highly accessible and scalable publishing techniques." In user-friendly terms, social media consists of online media platforms that allow members to publish information and engage in online discussion.

How does social media fit in?

Social media sites offer you the chance to grab your own piece of online real estate, so to speak. After you establish an account on a social media site, you can publish meaningful content that clearly communicates your message – who you are, what you do, what you like, and more. When you create your profile, comments, posts, articles, pictures, videos, reviews, and other content, interested visitors should be able to click through to your main site (website, blog, landing page, etc) to find out more. Social media offers online businesses a natural (called "organic") way to gain valuable traffic to your main site and the opportunity to engage them, leading to ever-expanding relationships and more sales.

Every time you create fresh content that contains a link to your main site, search engines love it – and your ranking is improved. A multitude of those "backlinks" significantly improves your ranking. Your goal is to be recognized for your chosen niche-specific "keywords" and achieve high enough ranking to be placed on their first page. Google (66%), Yahoo! (16%) and Bing (13%) account for the vast majority of search engines used, as of this writing. (It changes monthly.) For ease, we will primarily use Google throughout this book.

These terms and tools, and their uses, will be clarified in the pages that follow.

The online business success method

This book sorts through the clutter online and walks you through the step-by-step process of creating a dependable online business. Basically, you'll learn how to:

- Find an exciting niche product or service that is profitable.

- Set up the best technology and tools as simply and effectively as possible.

- Attract qualified potential customers to your site – and leverage social media.

- Convert your target prospects into sales, each and every day – for years to come!

We start with some very important exploration in order to find your perfect product or service. If you do this right, you'll enjoy the lucrative fruits of your labor. It won't happen overnight, but it *will* happen.

Success steps

The steps to success include:

- How to zero in on a profitable market niche you enjoy.

- Identify in-demand products to sell to your ideal customer.

- Build a dynamic web presence to sell your products or services – a website, blog, or landing page.

- Establish your social media presence and use it to expand your audience.

- Offer a free product in order to build a significant e-mail database.

✔*Outsourcing Tip: One online resource can show you how to effectively outsource many tasks to workers in the Philippines. They regularly pay talented, experienced workers as little as US $1.70 an hour, and as little as US $250 a month fulltime. Find out more here: http://www.replacemyself.com*

When you set up this method, you leverage social media and proven online marketing tools that attract natural (called "organic") traffic. When established with transparency and integrity, through the methods outlined in this book, your online business will generate continual income with minimal ongoing work on your part.

The beauty is, once you do it, you can repeat it. Set up multiple businesses as many times as you wish! Or expand your business by adding more products. I recommend that you do both in order to achieve diversity and increased income. Remember, as I mentioned in the Introduction, we will use the word "products" to mean both products and services.

Build Multiple Income Streams

Building your online business with this method will take you up an exciting learning curve. When you have traffic and customers, you can increase your income with two powerful leveraging techniques: Build multiple income streams in each business, and add more products.

Important: keep the products relevant to your topic and market niche. For example, if you're selling computer parts, then an ebook on blogging techniques (though perhaps interesting) is not relevant. But an ebook on new computer technology is relevant.

Build multiple income streams from multiple businesses

Repeat the method to create several online niche businesses (also with multiple products). These may be completely separate niches and target markets. However, it's advisable to start businesses that might appeal to the same niche. For example, if your first site sells products to dog lovers, then perhaps your second site might focus on home cleaning products. The connection here is that dog lovers are generally individuals and families who care about their home life. The people in your database may be interested in both, so you can kick-start your home cleaning products business.

Outsource and leverage your time

Setting up your business the right way, and promoting it both offline and online can be time-consuming. One solution is to outsource some of the more mundane tasks, such as posting promotional content to a wide variety of Internet sites (more on that later). The good news is that plenty of people are lined up to help out - individuals with skills and experience. Be sure to do your homework and ask about their capabilities before you engage them. You can find them online:

- Craigslist.org: http://www.craigslist.org
  For advertising your special job in your local market.

- RentACoder.com: http://www.rentacoder.com
  For specific projects.

- ODesk.com: http://www.odesk.com
  For link building.

Chapter One Highlights

- You can achieve online business success in the industry of your choice, doing something you love.

- Success Factor #1: Start with a proven, profitable method.

- Success Factor #2: Choose a profitable niche.

- Success Factor #3: Engage the right tools.

- Success Factor #4: Promote online and build your list.

- Your goal is to be recognized for your chosen "keywords" and achieve high enough ranking to be placed on the first page of top search engines.

- When your business is set up with transparency and integrity through the methods outlined in this book, it can generate continual income with minimal ongoing work on your part.

- Once you set it up, you can repeat it. Set up multiple businesses – as many times as you wish! Or expand your business by adding more products. Or both.

- Plenty of people are lined up to help out – individuals with skills and experience – through *outsourcing*.

Chapter Two

***

What Will You Sell?

How to research and choose the perfect product or service

If you already *have* your product or service, you'll want to skim this information anyway. It's an eye-opener for market research and competitive success insights.

If you *haven't* already decided what you're going to sell, then this may be THE most important material. It is literally the determinant of your online marketing success. For me, this is the fun part. It's like searching for, and finding, the missing piece of the puzzle.

Money – Love – Health – Happiness

In no certain order, people want money, love, health, and happiness. Find a niche or sub-niche in which you have special knowledge, expertise, or passion. A sub-niche of money might be "how to save money through couponing" or "how to make money as a ghost writer." Sub-niche information that offers solutions to problems or urgent needs in any of these four areas are likely to be the most profitable.

Of course, if you have expertise in gardening, there is a vast potential audience. Just Google 'garden problems' to see what people discuss online! For any topic or niche you're considering, it's wise to Google " _____ problems" – insert your niche in the blank – to find out what people need.

Mission critical: find a hot, solid niche

The very first thing to keep in mind is that you're looking for a product or service that appeals to an eager niche audience *and* is not already flooded with vendors offering it.

You're also looking for a profitable niche. What exactly is a niche? A niche is a subset or subcategory. Wal-Mart, for example, is a mass retailer selling a broad array of items that are in demand by the mass market. Their sporting goods aisle for fishermen carries only a very small selection of fishing flies. Bud's Fly Shop, on the other hand, is a small retailer that specializes in fly-fishing and carries a deep selection of flies. Bud's is a niche retailer. Wal-Mart is not.

On the Internet, remember, you're looking for a great niche product with:

- A definable audience to whom you will market,

- Enough sales potential to build a lucrative business,

- A market that is not too large. (A very large market puts you in competition with the giants.)

Many interesting and profitable niches are waiting for you online. The Internet and its retail marketplace is still in its infancy! Opportunity abounds. You are entering the market early, and by working smart, you *will* be successful.

So how do you find the niche product or service that's right for you?

What will you sell?

Your challenge is to identify a product or service that:

- You are excited about – even passionate. You want to enjoy this business!

- Solves your customers' problems, eases their pain, or provides them great pleasure.

- Has strong, steady demand (selling New Year's cards would not satisfy this one.)

- Is priced so that you can make a profit when you sell it – especially at a discount.

- Has a target audience that is fairly easy to penetrate.

- Is sought after by people who have enough discretionary spending money to buy it.

- Doesn't require you to make a large inventory investment upfront.

- Isn't inclined to be returned.

Whew! That's a long list, but a great many sources on the Internet now provide entrepreneurs with thousands of products that meet these objectives. Even if you don't have your own product, you can sell other companies' products. It's called "affiliate marketing" and we'll cover that later on. For now, just focus on finding your ideal niche.

Types of things to sell

When you boil it all down, you're really making a choice between selling three things:

1. Your services: Do you offer consulting? Landscaping? Jewelry repair?

2. Tangible products: Items that need to be shipped.

3. Information products: Valuable content that people seek through Internet search.

Note: From now on, for simplicity, I'll use only the term "product" to refer to both products and services. If you offer a service, it still applies.

Sell your services

It's likely that you already have a business "offline" that you own and/or operate. Perhaps you even have a website. If so, this book will help you leverage your base business, add profitable new revenue streams, and promote your business to increase sales.

Sell tangible products

Selling tangible goods may seem like a logical choice for someone who doesn't sell services. It's certainly the oldest and most common Internet business. Thousands of retailers are successful online and you can be successful, too. You can choose from several business models:

- Sell your own products.

- Sell others products, which they drop-ship.

- Sell products as an affiliate, earning a commission for each sale.

While physical products may seem more familiar, and may at first seem easier, they actually are not. Selling physical products entails inventory, shipping, returns and customer service. All those add up to money and time which lower your profits. Competition for physical product sales is fierce, with Amazon.com, Wal-Mart, and hundreds of thousands of retailers of all sizes and specialties on the Internet. Additionally, the Internet offers sites that do nothing but comparison price shop, which further squeezes profit margins on physical goods.

If you have your heart set on selling tangible goods, then this book will definitely help you overcome those obstacles. And, when you're ready, consider adding affiliate goods and information/digital products for diversification and multiple revenues streams – it's the name of the profit game!

Affiliate Marketing

Affiliate marketing has come a long way in the last few years and may be a great way to start out if you don't have your own products or services. Affiliate companies (more on these later) are free to join and it's also free to select the products they offer, grab your affiliate link, place it on your site, and begin to market them. If you already have a website or blog, adding affiliate products can quickly and easily provide your business with additional revenue.

Sell information products

I encourage you to think about selling *information products*. As we discussed, most people who search the Internet are looking for answers to their questions and solutions to problems. In the form of information, people are willing to pay for solutions. Usually, the best-selling information products:

- Make significantly more money than they cost.
- Save significantly more money than they cost.
- Solve an urgent or irritating problem.
- Save a lot of valuable time.
- Ease great pain.

Information products can be delivered digitally, so the cost to produce and deliver them can be miniscule. Many Internet sites offer services that enable you to create, record, and distribute your information products for low or no cost. We'll cover those later.

Information products last for years. When they provide *true value,* you can re-arrange the information, repurpose it, change the format and create follow-on products that offer great value and entice people to buy more lucrative packages.

Information products are NOT only e-books. Are you good at creating a plan or pattern for something? Have you found a great way to train or groom your dog? Have you discovered how to get kids to eat vegetables and/or other healthy recipes? You can record interviews with all kinds of willing subject matter experts (also known as SMEs).

These ideas, and thousands more, can be delivered as information products in a wide variety of formats:

- Ebooks.

- Reports.

- Instructional courses.

- How-To workbooks.

- Videos.

- Podcasts.

- Newsletters.

- Audio files (MP3 and the like).

- CDs.

- DVDs.

- Combination packages of the above.

If you have expertise in a subject area, you can make a name for yourself as an SME. *Stop for a moment* and *make a list* of the subject areas that you enjoy. You'll be surprised to discover that you know more than you might suspect. Are you a great cook? Do you have parenting tips? Do you love to grill? Even if you think it might be remote, put it on your list. Then from your list, Google each topic and see what's being discussed and what products are offered in that arena.

Alternatively, many experts offer resell rights to their digital information products, so if you don't want to start by creating original content, you can find others' products to sell! It's easy and we'll cover that in more detail later, too. But, be sure to choose an information topic that really interests you. You want to be excited about, and confident in, what you're doing!

Chapter Two Highlights

- Find a niche or sub-niche in which you have special knowledge, expertise, or passion.

- You're also looking for a *profitable* niche.

- Opportunity abounds. You're entering the market early and by working smart, you *will be* successful.

- Even if you don't have your own product, you can sell other companies' products.

- You're really making a choice between three things:

    1. Your services.

    2. Tangible products.

    3. Information products.

- Most people who search the Internet are looking for answers to their questions and solutions to problems. In the form of information products, people are willing to pay for solutions.

- Information products are delivered digitally, so the cost to produce them can be miniscule. And there are no worries about inventory, shipping, returns, etc.

Chapter Three

***

How to Choose a Niche

Find profitable niches and laser-targeted keywords that really work

Just like the boutique in the shopping center down the street, you want to offer something that's somewhat different, unique or better in some meaningful way. Offer something that's highly valued by your audience. This takes some research. Search online and use descriptive words and phrases – called keywords and key phrases – to uncover what's already abundantly available. From now on, for simplicity, I'll just use the term 'keywords' to cover both keywords and key phrases.

Don't skip lightly over this part of building your business! If you do, it's like building a house on sand. Make sure that you're building on firm foundation with thorough and meaningful research.

The Internet works brilliantly because *keywords* drive everything. They're the basis for every search engine that helps buyers find what they're looking for. If you don't start by strategizing, researching, and then using the right keywords, you may end up with a beautiful site, but no traffic and no sales. Keyword research is critical to your success. These exercises also orient you to tons of marketing insights and competitive advantages. Work smart by paying close attention to this. Have fun with it!

> ✔**Niche Tip:** *You're looking for an* **underserved** *niche, one that has more demand than supply.*

Where to find ideas: Start with trends

Now it's time to don your detective hat. Continue your market research by identifying trends and popular demand items in the media – both offline and online. Consider popular trends and *make a list of ideas*. The sources below will give you a very broad overview of topics and ideas of interest to the public.

Remember, you're looking for things that people are searching – products that solve peoples' problems and meet their needs and desires. Do as many of the following as necessary to get a feel for what's hot:

1. What trends are making the news? Be aware of stories and ads in offline newspapers, magazines, on TV and on the radio.

2. Scan 'Yahoo! Buzz' every day for top stories on the Internet: http://buzz.yahoo.com/

3. Use Google's 'Hot Trends' which identifies keywords people search on a daily basis: http://www.google.com/trends/hottrends

These will give you a pretty thorough snapshot. Next, more research will help you find specific products that sell.

How to brainstorm ideal keywords

Make a list of TEN ideas for products or services that come to mind and which you might be interested in selling. These should be things you enjoy and for which you have some specific knowledge or expertise.

> ✔**Keyword Tip:** *In order to find excellent keywords, pretend that you are your ideal customer, and that you are sitting at Google's search bar. What words will you use in your search?*

Get more specific: "The long tail"

It's important to narrow down your search to very specific keywords. For example, if you want to investigate how to offer your services as a fly fishing guide, a Google search for the term 'fishing' is too broad. That Google search will return a broad mix – like Wal-Mart's aisles – full of irrelevant things such as fishing rods, camping tents, and oars.

Your research needs to be more specific. Try "Fly Fishing Guide" – and then narrow your search more: "Fly Fishing Guide for Tennessee Streams." This specific, long phrase is called a 'long-tail' keyword and it's more likely to deliver the results you desire; sites that are closer to your specific idea.

Nailing the best search results

Since **keywords are everything** in this business, be sure to use the very best keyword search techniques possible. If you find that you're getting a lot of irrelevant results, even after you try more specific, long tail keywords, try these tips for Google searches (other search engines may have different tips and rules):

- *Exact Word:* Enter '+' before your keyword, such as '+toys' (note: no space after the +), to return only listings that include the +keyword.

- *Exact Phrase:* Enter your keywords in quotes, such as "safe toys for toddlers" to get return listings that use the phrase exactly as entered.

- *Similar Words:* Enter your keywords with '~', such as '~ safe toys' to get your word and all its synonyms.

- *Multiple Words:* Enter your keywords with 'OR' in between, such as 'safe toys or toys for toddlers', to get return listings that have either term.

- *Excluded Words:* Enter your keywords with '-' between, such as "safe toys – adult toys," to exclude any listings with the second term.

Strike a balance between specific enough, but not obscure

You'll know when you've found it because the search results will be more relevant and you'll see that the companies listed on the results pages could be your competitors. Click around and take note of what they sell, how they market and how they engage their audience.

Zero in on a niche that spends money

Food for thought: Imagine that you're considering selling a CD and workbook information package entitled: "How to Win in Bankruptcy." Whoa – your target audience likely has very little money to spend!

They are much more likely to search the Internet for this information for *free*. Run – don't walk. You could spend lots of time starting a business that is inherently less lucrative.

Rather, try this information package: "How to Franchise Your Successful Business." Now your target market is assumed to have a successful (i.e. profitable) business, with some cash available to pay you. And they're probably too busy running their business to spend their precious time searching for free information – they want immediate results. So, you may be on the right track. Find a niche that's more likely to spend money.

Drill down: What's selling?

Once you find popular items, you want to narrow your list to those hot products that also *sell* well. Let's do a bit more research to discover product ideas that are in demand and for which folks are paying hard-earned cash. Remember, this research is critical to find the right product and the right mix of supply and demand – much less work and more rewarding in the long run.

Check out Google Sponsored Ads

Find out what's selling through Google's sponsored ads. Type your product's long tail keywords in the Google search bar. When the results page comes up, look at the 'sponsored ads' on the right and at the top. These are likely competitors for that product – they are in business, paying ad dollars for those keywords, hoping to reach potential customers.

Check out eBay Pulse

Review eBay Pulse, a daily snapshot of current trends, hot picks, and cool stuff on eBay: http://pulse.ebay.com/Ebay is the granddaddy of all things sold online. If it's hot on eBay, it's hot everywhere.

Drill down further: Find sub-categories and sub-niches

Once you've surveyed the product landscape, narrow down your choices by getting a feel for what's in high demand. Remember, you're looking for popular items, but not oversupplied items.

Check out eBay Categories

Search for products on eBay, http://www.ebay.com/ then go to the Categories box and click on "All Categories". Each section has a "More" button to offer you a more detailed list. Click away. Search for products and more specialized, related products.

eBay Popular Products

To find the most popular products on eBay, search around their dedicated 'Popular' page: http://popular.ebay.com/ You'll want to click around here, too, to discover items that sell. Then click through to the Sellers' own page to check out your potential competition. After you check out the Sellers, search for them on Google – they may also offer their products on the Internet in general.

What's on Amazon?

Another way to check the niche: log on to Amazon http://www.amazon.com and search for books on your topic. The more you find there, the larger the audience.

✔**Niche Tip:** *Richard Legg offers enormous insight and tips to help you find a profitable niche in his video training program, "Niche Domination Secrets". Not free, but when your Internet business strategy rests on choosing a profitable niche, it may be worth the time and cost, as an investment, to get it right from the beginning: http://www.pureprofitsolutions.com/its/*

Make a final decision on your keywords

Now it's time to use your narrowed list of long tail keywords and find out how many times Google conducts searches for your potential customers. Everyone who searches your keyword is a potential customer!

Use Google AdWords' Keyword Tool to get the inside scoop on how many times your keywords are searched, globally and locally. Go to: https://adwords.google.com/select/KeywordToolExternal and type in your narrowed keyword list, one at a time. Google explains: "You can search for keyword ideas by entering a keyword related to your business or service or a URL (domain/website name) to a page containing content related to your business or service."

The results will provide the number of monthly searches conducted on this term, as well as suggestions for alternate wording and their search numbers. You're looking for keywords with at least 5,000 searches. The results will also give you an indicator of competition (low, medium, and high) as well as local search trends, among other indicators. It will even sort results by traffic and other ways … it's a fabulous tool!

Repeat your keyword or URL search until you're satisfied that you have identified the product that will meet the objectives listed above, and you have identified at least six great long tail keywords.

If you want to take this research to the next level, I advise two things:

- Google these keywords and check out the competition.

- Use Google's free Traffic Estimator tool to find out how much traffic your chosen keywords are likely to get: https://adwords.google.com/select/TrafficEstimatorSandbox

✔**Niche Tip:** *If you still aren't satisfied and want to search other places, see the Resources section at the end of this book for "Free Tools to Help Find Profitable Niches."*

Now you have your final product and keywords

Congratulations! You just accomplished one of the most important tasks for starting a successful, profitable, sustainable new online business. And you've learned a lot about the Internet, its communities and what people are searching for online. By laying this groundwork, you now have a strong foundation for your business. Carry on!

Chapter Three Highlights

- The Internet works brilliantly because *keywords* drive everything. They're the basis for every search engine algorithm that helps buyers find what they're looking for.

- Keyword research is critical to your success.

- You're looking for an *underserved* niche, one that has more demand than supply.

- Make a list of TEN ideas for products or services that come to mind, and which you might be interested in selling. These should be things you enjoy, and for which you have some specific knowledge or expertise.

- Research will help you find specific products that sell. To start your research, use Google.

- If you find that you're getting a lot of irrelevant re-sults, try more specific, long tail keywords.

- Find a niche that spends money.

- Once you've surveyed the product landscape, nar-row down your choices by getting a feel for what's in high demand.

- Use your narrowed list of keywords and find out how many times Google conducts searches for your potential customers.

- Repeat your search until you're satisfied that you have identified the product that will meet your ob-jectives, and you have identified at least six great long tail keywords.

Chapter Four

***

Create Your Brand

Profile your ideal customer, know your competition and brand yourself

From this point forward, the effectiveness of everything you do, including the site you build, the content you write, the products you offer, the sales you make – and everything else – depends on how well you know and appeal to your ideal customer. Take a few minutes NOW to profile them and write these things down. You will refer to this written ideal customer profile later as you make decisions about topics to cover and products you choose. If you don't do this, your entire business may be off-target and you could spend months and years chasing, with no results.

Spend critical, clear-thinking time NOW to define your ideal customer profile, specific to the niche you chose:

- List their top 30 needs.
- List 20 unique problems they face.

- List 10 of their topic-related likes and 10 dislikes.

- List 40 products they buy.

- List 25 questions they have – answers to which are information topics they would be eager to read.

That's a good start. While you go through this exercise, add anything else that comes to mind that you feel is important to them. Save this profile and add to it from time to time as you learn more about them. This list is gold for your business:

✔**Helpful Tool Tip: Not free, but affordable, and a great investment**

Hot Item Finder

"An easy way to find the best selling products on eBay in only minutes."
– HotItemFinder http://www.hotitemfinder.com/

Keyword Elite

*"Traffic is **not** the key to making money on the Internet. You have to have the RIGHT traffic. Traffic that is full of 'buyers'...." I'm sure you would agree that there is a HUGE difference between a browser and a buyer. 98% of people THINK they're getting the right kind of traffic, which leaves 2%. Of those 2%, 1% gets only a small portion of the right kind of traffic, and only the top 1% of all online marketers actually know how to get this massive money making "buyer" traffic." – Keyword Elite http://www.keywordelite.com*

Brand yourself

Branding your online business will help set you apart from your competitors. When you establish a memorable visual appeal, as well as a meaningful and compelling message, your audience will react positively and help you by passing your information on to others in their network. Books are written on branding, so this is simply an introduction to get you started:

1. Write down your mission statement (include keywords if you can and how you help others). Example: "Google's mission is to organize the world's information and make it universally accessible and useful."

2. Create a memorable logo that's in line with your business niche.

3. List "must-have" benefits to your customers (such as solutions to their problems and answers to their questions).

4. Choose a page design that you can use on all pieces and sites you create. Pay special attention to layout, graphics, colors, fonts and style.

5. Have a professional photo of yourself taken.

6. Write a bio that highlights your expertise and brings out the personal you. Add information about yourself outside of your work life. For example, "She loves to grow roses and read mystery novels."

7. Use all of the above consistently on each of your sites and profiles.

Know your online competition

Knowing how you compare to your competitors will give you the power to shine when visitors reach your site. Go back to Google and search for a few of your best keywords. Find businesses that look like they compete with you (exclude directory sites, etc.).

Take time now to familiarize yourself with these sites. Your one competitive goal is to be better than they are in some meaningful way. That might include any number of competitive advantages such as:

- Better product selection.
- More interesting, accessible and updated content.
- Easier site navigation.
- "Stickiness" – you offer something that makes your visitors want to stay on your site.
- Freebies.

Before you actually design and build your site, spend some time reviewing your competitors' sites. Do they:

- Grab your attention within 2-3 seconds?
- Clearly and quickly convey the benefits of what they offer?
- Establish their credibility?
- Keep you interested by offering intriguing content?
- Stimulate your desire to learn more?
- Persuade you to take action?

What will you do better than they do? Make a list of these thoughts now, as you review your competition. You will refer to them later as you decide what to put on your home page and the supporting pages. From time to time, go back and check out your competition. The

Internet is constantly changing and you want to stay on top with competitive strategies!

> ✔*Social Media Groups Tip:* "*Search for interactive social media groups in order to expand your online presence. When you sign up for a group, you can post a question and get responses. Using social media in this way is like accessing one big marketing focus group. Go ahead – bounce ideas around and ask for feedback. Find a group that is centered on the topic or product you're considering. For instance, find a group of Internet entrepreneurs. Then ask them what they think of the idea. Like this: "I'm thinking about starting a business online to sell my handcrafted sterling silver salad tongs. Who would be my biggest competition? How would I market to potential customers online?" Lots of people are likely to offer suggestions and new ideas that your research didn't uncover.*

Google Groups

"Google Groups is all about helping users connect with people, access information, and communicate effectively over email and on the web." – Google http://groups.google.com/

Brainstorm ideal domain names

Have you noticed that we researched products and keywords before we even mentioned domain names? That's a deliberate strategic move.

Domain names that *include keywords* are more likely to be ranked higher. Search engines assume that the name of your site is relevant to the topic of your site, so in the search algorithms, they give more weight to the domain name, and thus your ranking - how high up you rank in the results pages. Makes sense, doesn't it?

The domain name is only one of many factors used in search algorithms (and algorithms also vary among search engines.) It's a very important factor.

So now, let's brainstorm domain names. Keep these things in mind – your domain name should be:

- As short as possible. Try for fewer than five syllables.
- Memorable.
- Keyword-oriented.

Choose a domain name registrar

Plenty of places online offer domain name search tools. Some may limit the number of times you may search, others do not. I personally like to work with registrars that offer live support – not just email ticket support (in which you must submit a request for help through the site's email "ticket" system and are given a ticket number). Later, when I have a hosting or billing question, or an issue that might delay me in managing my business (or, heaven forbid, my site goes down), my time is much more valuable than saving $2-5 upfront.

Other things to look for when choosing a domain registrar:

- The company offers hosting as well as registration.
- Their site should be user-friendly, with intuitive tabs and clear instructions.
- They offer free domain name transferring capabilities.
- They offer email attached to the site.
- They offer website building capabilities.

✔**\$\$ Saving Tip:** *Before you checkout and finalize your purchase of the domain name and hosting package on the registrar site, Google "GoDaddy (or Dotster) coupon code," or "GoDaddy promotion code." You'll find a plethora of discount offers on the Internet. Just be sure that it hasn't yet expired. Jot down the code and enter it in the appropriate box at checkout.*

✔**Social Media Community Tip: *After you have your website,*** *Dotster.com offers a unique a la carte (it costs extra) social media service called Dotster Connect, allowing more advanced online businesses to create its own social network community; an "online network of customers, employees or partners – a place where people can collaborate using social media and social networking applications such as forums, groups, media sharing, polls, awards, articles and newsletters. Dotster Connect is an advanced Web 2.0 platform for companies looking to create their own community website. Dotster Connect is a customizable solution that includes strategy and planning, website design, development, site hosting, and on-going maintenance. Dotster offers four different packages to fit all business sizes and budgets." –Dotster Connect http://www.dotster.com/connect/*

Two great companies that offer all the above at the most reasonable prices are:

- Dotster.com: www.dotster.com
- GoDaddy.com: www.godaddy.com

✔**Domain Registration Tip:** *Both of these registrars have excellent* **live** *customer support. So if you're new to all this and it seems a bit overwhelming, relax – really! Just give them a call and they will take their time to help you and explain, step by step, what you need to do. Ask as many questions as you wish. Their job is to help you until you're satisfied!*

How to search for your domain name

Search for .com extensions only. They are the most-used, and perceived as the most legitimate – especially for a business. It may take some creativity and patience to find a great name, but it's well worth it in the long run. Don't cave in on this point. People expect to type in .com extensions. If yours is something else, you *will* lose traffic.

✔**Domain Name Tip:** *One insight should help make your name search easier: Start with your most inspiring keyword/phrase, then add a common, industry-specific modifier extension. For example, my search for "www.fishingflies.com" revealed that it was not available. However, my next search for "FishingFliesMarket.com" delighted me – it was available! The "market" modifier would be great if you intend to sell fishing flies on your site. Now you have a name that makes sense, is five syllables (not too bad!) and is keyword-specific. This will help your online store achieve higher search engine rankings faster.*

Avoid hyphenated names. They usually aren't easy to remember and your target customers will quickly go to other businesses listed on the search results page.

Granted, the short, easy, and top-of-mind names are probably already taken. When the domain name search tool suggests alternate choices, consider them, but don't waste too much time. My experience is that those suggestions are rarely, if ever, excellent choices.

Confirm your choice

To affirm that you have a winner, search for the domain name in Google, using spaces in between the words. For example, search for "fishing flies market." What do you find? Are the results on the page relevant to your intended business? Does another company with that name already exist?

Next, your objective is to be reasonably sure that the name you've chosen isn't already in use by another business. Search for your chosen name as a trademark on The United States Patent and Trademark Office, online at http://www.uspto.gov - the official site of the national trademarks database. If you don't find it, then you will want to take it one step further and search your state's website for the Secretary of State's Office in order to clear it at the state or local level. Ultimately, you may want to engage an attorney to finalize your name selection as you file documents necessary to establish your company's entity (such as LLC or corporation, etc.)

To secure a trademark, you may wish to engage a service to research thoroughly and file a trademark application. One such service, Trademark Express, with very reasonable prices and offices in California and Washington D.C., can be found online at http://www.tmexpress.com

Congratulations! You're way ahead of most online businesses and on your way to building value. I hope that you're getting a solid feel for your market, its audience of potential customers, your competition, and what your niche wants.

Stake your online real estate now!

As I mentioned earlier, it's very early in the overall scheme of things online. The Internet and social media is in its infancy. You now have an opportunity to 'claim to your online real estate'. Establish accounts *in your name* with key online and social media platforms before your brand and/or your name is taken by someone else. Once they're taken, they will not be available again. You have this one chance to establish a full portfolio with your unique brand – *do it now!*

Chapter Four Highlights

- The effectiveness of everything you do, including the site you build, the content you write, the products you offer, the sales you make – and everything else – depends on how well you know and appeal to your ideal customer.

- Branding your online business will set you apart from your competitors.

- Knowing how you compare to your competitors will give you the power to shine when visitors reach your site.

- Your one competitive goal is to be better than they are in some meaningful way.

- Use social media groups for market research – it's like accessing one big marketing focus group.

- Choose a domain name that *includes keywords* – it is more likely to be ranked higher by search engines.

- Work with domain name registrars that offer live

support – not just email ticket support.

- You now have an opportunity to claim your online real estate. Establish accounts in your name with top online and social media platforms – before they're taken by someone else.

Chapter Five

***

Create Your Online Presence

Start with a killer website and a magnetic blog

Choose one type of site as your home base, usually a website or blog. This will be the hub of your online business, and the site that connects everything you do. Your social media accounts will link to this site, and vice-versa. This would be the one place you send people, if you had to choose only one.

Website or blog?

What do you start first, a website or blog? It's quite a common question, and one which begs another question; "What are your goals?" Do you intend to:

- Sell products that you already own?
- Establish an affiliate marketing business – selling

others' products?

- Make money from paid advertising that others place on your site (more about that later)?

Build a blog

Just in case you're not familiar with blogs, they are software platforms that act as journals, wherein the blogger (that's you) can write online journal entries (called "posts") and publish them to the Internet. Blogs are important for SMEs (Subject Matter Experts) to write and share items of interest to their target audience – their prospective customers.

Blogs are one of the original social media tools, enabling visitors to interact socially by commenting on blog posts and adding value to the discussion with their own ideas. Visitors love to comment and include a link to their own website, blog, or social media page, because these "backlinks" help their search engine rankings. So, to encourage visitor interaction, blog about topics of high interest, including controversial subjects. And be sure to ask a thought-provoking question at the end of your post, inviting visitor comments.

Different blog platforms offer a variety of advantages. Choose among sites such as Wordpress, Movable Type, Blogger, Typepad, etc. My personal favorite is Word-Press, due to its wide functionality and ease of use, and it's free. For more information about pros and cons of top blog platforms, see Melanie Nelson's blog post: http://www.bloggingbasics101.com/2009/01/choosing-a-blogging-platform/

GoDaddy.com (not free) and Dotster.com (not free) can accommodate both websites and blogs that require hosting, such as WordPress.com (free) and MovableType.com (free for individuals). Blogs that do not require external hosting include Blogger.com (free) and TypePad.com (not free).

If you need hosting for your blog platform, purchase the keyword-rich .com domain name and add hosting. Ask about their package for hosting multiple domain names if you intend to create multiple businesses. All blog platforms offer help, tutorials and detailed how-tos. But they aren't difficult. With a bit of instruction, you'll catch on quickly – like millions before you!

✔***Keyword Tip:*** *"Keyword rich" means that you should choose about three different keywords for each page. Then use those keywords about 3% of the time – for every 100 words, use each keyword three times. The best places to use them are in headings and subheadings. Also italicize them. Search engines place more emphasis on the first 200 words on the page, so it helps to locate them in your text near the top of the page.*

✔***Keyword Tip:*** *After you populate your site with keyword-rich content, use this free tool to check the keyword density: http://tools.seobook.com/general/keyword-density/ If you haven't achieved the 3% goal on your top long tail keywords, go back and rewrite some of the content and check it again. This step is really important! When you achieve 3% density, search engines give you a higher rank for those keywords.*

Blog fresh content

Blogging is a great way to create fresh content that search engines love. It takes a real commitment to write and post new articles on a regular basis – usually two to three posts each week. Posts should be between 250-400 words because readers get impatient if they're longer. And your posts *must* contain those strategically chosen long tail keywords in order to attract your ideal customer. In fact, before you write, choose three to five keywords *first*, much the same way you chose them to find your niche. Then write the article and use the keywords in the headline, subhead, italicized and bolded throughout the body. Make sure that the content flows easily, using the keywords as naturally as possible.

See how nicely this is starting to fit together? Using specifically chosen keywords, and derivations of them, is the single most important thing you do as an Internet marketer.

The content of your blog is your business' message – but *not* used as advertising or promotion. Instead, write about helpful, insightful, and valuable information. Remember that people search the Internet for answers to solve a problem or fulfill a need. Make a list of topics that work together to help people learn about your niche. Plan your content so that it gives meaningful or entertaining information.

Your blog should *not*:

- Sound like an advertisement.

- Post press releases.

- Display products catalog-style.

If you find yourself writing promotional copy, stop and study popular blogs that get high ranking on Google. Find them by simply typing your topic and the word "blog" in the Google search bar, for instance: "watercolor blog" (if your business sells watercolor supplies).

Be sure to ask a thought-provoking question at the end of your post, inviting readers to submit comments and engage in the discussion. This is how you begin to build real relationship and community. Your blog serves as a hub to inspire and recognize others who are interested in your niche!

✔**SEO Blogger Tip:** *SEO Blogger is a free tool that works with any blog publishing software and allows you to find the most sought-after keywords for your subject without ever leaving your blog editing screen. The tool sits alongside whatever blog publishing software you're using so you can do keyword research and optimize your posts as you write. Then, simply hit "Publish" – and you're done! Compare keywords instantly to find out which ones pack the most SEO punch. (For example, should you write an article about "sustainable buildings" or "green buildings"?) Automatically track how many times you've used each chosen keyword in your post."*

Get SEO Blogger here: http://labs.wordtracker.com/seo-blogger/

Note: SEO Blogger requires the Firefox browser http://getfirefox.com

Behind the blog

On the technical side, use these features to help ensure that your blog is recognized and highly ranked by search engines:

- *Assign each post to a category* and keep the number of categories to a minimum. Think of them like chapters in a book.

- *Create tags.* Tags complement categories. Think of them like the headings in a chapter of a book. They help search engines find your content.

- *Use the automated RSS* (Real Simple Syndication) feed function. RSS feeds publish your content in a standardized format.

- *Use social bookmarking* such as Stumbleupon.com, Technorati.com, and Digg.com to get backlinks to your content quickly. (More about this later.)

RSS feeds allow you to automate the broadcast of your content. Individuals who are interested in your topic and want to receive your future posts can subscribe to your RSS feed using Outlook's RSS Reader or Google Reader. They will then automatically receive your content when you publish it. RSS feeds can also be integrated into your accounts on social media platforms such as Facebook, LinkedIn Groups, and Twitter. For specific details, see the instructions on each site.

According to Wikipedia, "Social bookmarking is a method for Internet users to share, organize, search, and manage bookmarks of web resources. Unlike file sharing, the resources themselves aren't shared, merely bookmarks that reference them."

"Monetize" your blog platform

Many folks now use a blog as an Internet store. Blogging platforms were not originally created to be as flexible as websites to sell products and conduct business online. However, if you're willing and able to do a little extra work on your blog, added functionality through 'plugins' are now available, at little or no cost, to provide specific functionality that meets your needs.

For its versatility and easy customization, I highly recommend using the WordPress (WP) blogging platform (http://www.wordpress.com) A WordPress account is free, and gives you access to everything you need to set up and use your blog. To create an online store in your WordPress blog, several plugins are readily available. They offer a lot of options, ranging from PayPal checkout to social media integration. Search for e-commerce plugins on WordPress.com here: http://wordpress.org/extend/plugins/search.php?q=ecommerce

WordPress eCommerce

One WordPress plugin for conducting e-commerce is highly recommended and has social media capabilities: WP e-Commerce Plugin. "Install WP e-Commerce in minutes. Like all well-designed plugins, WP e-Commerce integrates seamlessly with the WordPress Update System – so when you upload a new product, the world knows about it. WP e-Commerce makes it easy for you to accept payments online, integrating with Google Checkout, PayPal, Authorize.net, Payment Express and many other trusted payment processors...."

The basic WP e-Commerce plugin may be downloaded here: http://www.instinct.co.nz/e-commerce/

Build a website

A typical website has a home page with attention-getting headlines and information. The content of your home page must be keyword rich. The home page also offers tabs to several sub-pages for more specific topics of interest.

Both domain hosts mentioned above (GoDaddy.com and Dotster.com) offer website building tools at quite reasonable prices. Several packages are available depending on your needs. They offer all the tools you need to set up shop, including multiple page sites, site building tools, email, shopping carts, etc.

Generally, steps to build your own site are detailed in the package (and remember, they have live help):

- Choose a site design from hundreds of template choices.

- Customize it with your choice of layout design, colors, elements and images.

- Use webmaster tools they provide in order to keyword optimize your site for search engines.

You can build your new site yourself or you can have someone build it for you. Both companies offer this service, or many website designers will create it for you. If you take this route, be sure that you've planned it very carefully. Compare it to your competitors' sites. Does it have all the elements you feel are important? Is it better in some meaningful way? Lack of planning quickly drives up your costs!

✔**Website Building Tip:** *If you're building your site yourself, access free graphics, buttons, banners, fonts, borders and text at CoolText.com: http://www.cooltext.com*

Make your site "sticky"

"Sticky" means that once a visitor lands on your page, they want to stay and look around. Here are some tips on how to grab and hold your visitors' attention and create a sticky site:

- Attention-grabbing headline and subhead – within two to three seconds.

- Relevant and interesting pictures and images.

- Easy site navigation.

- *Clear and compelling "Call to Action!"* (State exactly what you want them to do.)

- White space around important text.

- Authentic, original, meaningful information.

- Long tail keywords in headline, subheads, images, and content – italicized and bolded.

- Articles related to the niche topic.

- White papers and Reports.

- Video, Audio, Podcasts on "How-To" topics.

- Blog – new content three times per week – with visitor comment capability.

- Discussion forum.

- Online press kit and examples of your media coverage.

- Bookmarks.

- RSS feeds.

- Opt-in email emphasizing "no share" privacy policy – with an autoresponder.

- Security emphasized on every page.

- Traffic stats for monitoring.

Add comment capability

Disqus Comments is a comment system and moderation tool for your site. This service lets you add community management and social web integrations to any site on any platform. Hundreds of thousands of sites, from small blogs to large publications, use Disqus Comments for their discussion communities. Try a demo and sign up free: http://www.disqus.com/

Add a forum

Engage your visitors and make your site stickier by adding a forum. Lefora offers free forums to imbed in your site. There is nothing to download, and no limit on the number of forums you can create. With the free version, you get 10GB of monthly bandwidth. On public forums, every topic has a button that will allow your members to share a link to the topic on social networking sites like Facebook, Twitter, and Myspace. http://www.lefora.com/

Examples of award winning sites

Now that you've chosen your niche, identified long tail keywords, registered and hosted your domain name, and covered basic site elements, it's time to get really creative! Have you noticed other sites that you really like? It's okay to use them as inspiration for building your own site's look, feel, and functionality. But be original – copyright infringement can be very costly.

The Web Marketing Association showcases its WebAward Competition winners in 96 industries. They set the standard of excellence for all website development. Search for winning sites in your industry or niche here: http://www.webaward.org/winners.asp

Site design, content, and quality guidelines

Whether you're using a website or blog, it's your home base, and we'll refer to it simply as your "site." So let's focus on how to make that site the best it can be – a very important first impression and a competitive advantage.

Your site must be "search engine friendly." This means that search engines will love the way it's built, and will easily identify the keywords you incorporate into the content. "Search Engine Optimization" (SEO) is an art and science unto itself. People make careers of nothing but SEO work. But if you follow some simple guidelines, you'll have a site that'll do the job.

What's a good way to ensure that your site is search engine friendly? Follow Google's design, content and quality guidelines: http://www.google.com/support/webmasters/bin/answer.py?hl=en&answer=35769

> ✔ **Site Design Tip:** *Internet surfers make snap decisions about whether or not a site is worthy of their time. Once they land on your site, you have about two to three seconds to grab your visitors' attention and interest, intriguing them to stay on the site and explore. Your headline and graphics are your most powerful elements. Remember, they may come to your site through any page, so this tip applies to all of your pages.*

Start with a website and a blog

Ideally, it's best to start a website and add a blog to it. Once the website is functioning as your online store, the blog and its fresh, unique, and keyword-rich content will serve to attract your ideal customers. The combination is dynamic – if you have the time to blog regularly.

Chapter Five Highlights

- Choose one type of site as your home base – usually a website or blog. This will be the hub of your online business and the site that connects everything you do.

- Your social media accounts will link to this site, and vice-versa.

- Blogs are important for SMEs (Subject Matter Experts) to write and share articles of interest with their target audience who are their prospective ideal customers.

- "Keyword rich" means that you should choose about three different long tail keywords for each page. Then use those keywords about 3% of the time; for every 100 words, use each keyword three times.

- Post new articles on a regular basis – usually two to three posts each week. Posts should be between 250-400 words because readers get impatient if they're longer.

- Write about helpful, insightful and valuable information. Remember that people search the Internet for answers to solve a problem or fulfill a need.

- If you find yourself writing promotional copy, stop and study popular blogs that get high ranking on Google.

- RSS feeds allow you to automate the broadcast of your content.

- Many folks now use a blog as an Internet store.

- A typical website has a home page with attention-getting headlines and information. Make your site "sticky" and search engine friendly.

- Follow Google's design, content, and quality guidelines.

- Ideally, it's best to start a website and add a blog to it.

Chapter Six

***

Help Search Engines Find Your Site

Search Engine Optimization (SEO) demystified: The key to getting traffic

When building your site, be sure that it's optimized for your long tail niche keywords and that it incorporates other tactics which help search engines find it.

Search engines' goal

Search engines' ultimate goal is to make it easy to find information relevant to the search topic. They are very sophisticated and their "algorithms" for search are highly confidential. Many SEO professionals study search engine behavior and offer these tips for what the search engines deem important when ranking content:

- Keywords in the domain name.
- Keywords in the content pages.

- Keywords in titles and subtitles.
- Keywords with emphasis – such as italics, bold, highlighted.
- External links (backlinks) to your site.
- Your site's age.

SEO guide

One favorite guide to SEO has been downloaded *free* over a million times. Offered by SEOmoz.org, "The Beginner's Guide to Search Engine Optimization (SEO) is an in-depth tutorial on how search engines work. It covers the fundamental strategies that make websites search engine friendly. To download your copy of the world's most read guide on SEO, join the community of SEOmoz PRO members."

The content covers:

- How search engines operate.
- How people interact with search engines.
- Why search engine marketing is necessary.
- The basics of search engine friendly design and development.
- Keyword research.
- How usability, experience, and content affect rankings.
- Growing popularity and links.
- Search engine tools and services.
- Myths and misconceptions about search engines.
- Measuring and tracking success.

Download your copy here:

http://www.seomoz.org/dp/download-the-pdf-version-of-the-beginners-guide-to-seo

✔*Anchor Text Tip: Use "Anchor Text" to improve your search results. Every time you insert an image or a link into your content, ensure that you attach anchor text containing your keywords. The image insertion tool provides this capability. Anchor text is recognized by search engines and will help your SEO. For example, instead of adding a link that looks like this: "http://www.yourdomainname.com" using anchor text will "rename" the link and add your keyword so that it looks like this: "watercolor tutorial." The search engine will recognize the underlying link and the keyword, giving you a double-whammy for SEO.*

Test your site. Did you succeed?

Professional site designers use tools to measure how well the site is optimized for search and so can you. Try this free tool to scan your site and get detailed results at WebsiteGrader http://www.websitegrader.com If you didn't score so well, go back and rewrite the content, including your keywords in the headings, subheads or text – with italics and bolding. Then go back to WebsiteGrader and test again. Repeat until you're satisfied that search engines will recognize your content for those critical keywords. It's important.

One-stop store setup

Yahoo! Merchant Solutions' claim: "Yahoo!'s Small Business offers PC Magazine's Editor's Choice 'Merchant Solutions' as a complete e-commerce package for selling online and bringing your business onto the Internet. Yahoo! Merchant Solutions is perfect for an entrepreneur – the small business that wants an online presence. Some of the features include: an easy to use ecommerce wizard and product details page, customizable store design, payment processor of credit debit and Pay-Pal, free marketing and promotion of your store through a variety of Yahoo! powered tools and partnerships, free traffic driving technologies, order processing and shipping, web analytics and tracking, inventory management, and first rate security. Yahoo!'s Small Business provides this one stop shop for merchants to sell online easily, affordably, and successfully." http://smallbusiness.yahoo.com/

✔**Branding Tip:** *By establishing and integrating your message into several online and social media platforms, you establish your brand. Be sure to create consistency in the look, feel, and sound bites among your various platforms. Your brand is an important component of your niche marketing strategy. When you convey a meaningful and important message, attract targeted traffic and build trust - your brand becomes increasingly valuable.*

✔*Conversation Tip: One very important fundamental:* *When you blog, post comments, write articles, and generally engage in social media conversations,* **never** *"push" your message or make a sales pitch. Social media is not advertising or promotion.* **Period***. If you have affiliate products, just offer reviews and your link. People* **will** *click through. Don't "push-market." You must naturally engage in social discussion and allow others to ask for more information about you – and your business. By listening first, you will learn how others do it. Follow their example.*

Chapter Six Highlights

- When building your site, be sure that it's optimized for your long tail niche keywords and incorporates other tactics that help search engines find it.

- Professional site designers use tools to measure how well the site is optimized for search and so can you.

- By establishing and integrating your message into several online and social media platforms, you establish your brand. Be sure to create consistency in the look, feel, and sound bites among your various platforms.

- When you blog, post comments, write articles, and generally engage in social media conversations, *never* "push" your message or make a sales pitch.

Chapter Seven

***

Add More Revenue Streams

More easy ways to make money from your website

The oldest and easiest income generator for your site is advertising. It requires little to no effort on your part, and as your traffic grows, so does the money you make. You've seen them in many forms, including:

- Banner ads.

- Text ads.

- Pop-up ads.

- Affiliate ads.

Let's dive in and explore how they work. You can decide which, if any, are right for your site.

CPM ad revenue

CPM stands for "Cost Per Thousand." The pay scale depends upon the number of unique visitors on your site each month. CPM ads were the original strategy to monetize a website in the early Internet days. They are easy and can deliver significant income if you have a high volume of traffic. However, the pay rates are as low as a nickel per thousand unique visitors. So, you'd need to have two million unique visitors in order to make $100 a month! Popup ads may pay more – perhaps as high as $2 per thousand, requiring 50,000 visitors to make $100 a month. But visitors really dislike popups so I don't recommend it.

Some CPM ad networks pay better for very high quality niche sites. If you qualify and wish to pursue it, try Google's CPM program or:

- Advertising.com http://www.advertising.com

- TribalFusion.com http://www.tribalfusion.com

- ValueClick.com http://www.valueclick.com

- RightMedia.com http://www.rightmedia.com

- AdBrite.com http://www.adbrite.com

CPC ad revenue

CPC stands for "Cost Per Click." The pay scale depends upon the number of times visitors click on the ad on your site each month. They are also easy and the payout rates are higher than CPM. If you have traffic from a highly targeted niche with lots of advertisers, CPC ads may work well for you. Try Google AdSense or other CPC networks:

- YPN – Yahoo! Publisher Network
  http://advertising.yahoo.com/publisher/index

- BidVertiser.com http://www.bidvertiser.com

- Chitika.com http://www.chitika.com
- Clicksor http://www.clicksor.com
- Kontera http://www.kontera.com

CPA ad revenue

CPA stands for "Cost Per Action." The pay scale depends upon your visitors clicking through and taking an action, which could be purchasing something, but not always. Some CPA ads pay you for visitors who click, or for visitors who take some action, such as to register for a report or a free trial.

Affiliate programs are CPA-based. When you sign up as an affiliate marketer, you get paid when someone clicks through on the affiliate link and makes a purchase. In addition to Commission Junction and Clickbank, some of the best CPA networks include:

- Epic Direct http://www.epicdirectnetwork.com/
- Adknowledge Affiliate http://www.hydragroup.com/
- ClickBooth http://www.clickbooth.com/
- MAXBounty http://www.maxbounty.com/
- COPEAC http://www.copeac.com/
- neverblue http://www.neverblue.com/

Find your own advertisers

It may take some work, but it's an option! AdBrite.com (http://www.adbrite.com) gives you the opportunity to offer your space for your own price. Look for this option on almost any major ad network.

Sell others' products

Earlier, I mentioned that you can sell products from others if you don't have products of your own. Or, you can sell others' products in *addition* to your own. Affiliate marketing is the term commonly used to describe the relationship between the wholesaler of the products and the retailer (you).

Sell affiliate products

Signing up as an affiliate marketer to sell others' products is generally free. When you sign up (which should take only a few minutes), you become a marketer of the specific niche products that you choose, earning a commission for each sale. Commissions can be quite lucrative, especially for information products – as high as 75%.

Many companies act as a sort of affiliate product store, supplying you with the products and support services you need to automate this function. Tens of thousands of different products are available.

Top affiliate marketing companies

Two great companies have been in business for years, and run quite smoothly and successfully:

- ClickBank – http://www.clickbank.com/
- Commission Junction – www.commissionjunction.com

They want you to be successful, because when you're successful, they are too. So they offer a lot of training information, advice and resources to make affiliate marketing simple and quick, even for beginners.

After you sign up, search for niche products by keywords, grab your affiliate links and insert them into your online page. When you insert the links be sure to add descriptive text that promotes the product, *and use your long tail keywords*. Remember, this text will be crawled by search engines and will help your ideal customers find you.

Sell your own products through affiliate networks

If you have your own products to sell, you can also offer them to other affiliate marketers who earn a commission when they sell them. This can all be handled by the affiliate companies mentioned above. Now *you're* the wholesaler and other marketers are the retailers.

Start by determining the retail price of your product and the percentage commission you will offer. Take a minute to search the affiliate company's vendor/advertiser listings for similar products. You want to set your price and commission competitively.

Next, create a sales page that describes your product and what it will do for the ultimate buyer. Use keywords here, too, and be sure it sounds enticing. Sales will be affected either positively or negatively by the tone and call to action. Take a look at other successful product pages for examples. Submit this page to the affiliate company for approval. They will provide payment links for you to place on your site page.

Now, you can sit back and wait for affiliate marketers to find your product, *or* – which I highly recommend – you can promote your affiliate product and the commission in the same ways that you promote your site. (More on this later.)

Chapter Seven Highlights

- The oldest and easiest income generator for your site is advertising.

- CPM stands for "Cost Per Thousand." The pay scale depends upon the number of unique visitors on your site each month.

- CPC stands for "Cost Per Click." The pay scale depends upon the number of times visitors click on their ad on your site each month.

- CPA stands for "Cost Per Action." The pay scale depends upon your visitors clicking through and taking an action.

- Affiliate programs are CPA-based. When you sign up as an affiliate marketer, you get paid when someone clicks through on the affiliate link and makes a purchase.

- Signing up as an affiliate marketer to sell others' products is generally free. Commissions can be quite lucrative – as high as 75%.

- If you have your own products to sell, you can also offer them to other affiliate marketers who earn a commission when they sell them.

Chapter Eight

***

Sell Digital Products

How to offer lucrative digital information products

It's quite exciting to learn that the Internet offers volumes of digital information that you can purchase very inexpensively and resell from your site. They come in many forms, as discussed earlier, including: e-books, reports, videos, podcasts, etc.

You can resell them or even *give them away* as free bonuses! Anything of value that is free will certainly help get and *keep* the attention of your target audience. In fact, your keywords can then include "free" – which will command even more traffic.

Digital products – purchase them inexpensively!

ClickBank.com and ResellRightsWeekly.com memberships are free, and known for offering high quality PLR (Private Label Rights) products. I've also found fresh digital products by searching Google for "PLR Store" – but please, be discerning when you search for PLR goods. Make sure they're high quality before you buy. (More about PLR below).

You can also find them on eBay.com. I've purchased them there. Since they are placed in a deep location, here are the exact steps to find them:

1. Go to http://www.ebay.com

2. Click "Categories"

3. Click "Everything Else"

4. Click "Information Products"

5. Click "Other"

6. In the search bar on the "Other" page, enter "Resell Rights" and hit the green search button

You now have a list of products that contain hundreds – even thousands – of items with resell rights, many for under $20. Make sure that you know what kind of rights you're getting – RR, MRR, or PLR.

What is RR, MRR, and PLR – and why is that important?

These abbreviations differentiate the kind of rights you buy. It's important to understand the difference between them, as they enable you, as a retailer, to do different things:

- RR = Resale Rights. You have the right to resell the product *as is* only. You cannot change the product in any way, and you cannot pass along the right to resell the product.

- MRR = Master Resale Rights. You have the right to resell the product *as is* only (same as RR). You cannot change the product, *but* you *can* pass along the right to resell the product.

- PLR = Private Label Rights. You have the right to resell the product. You *can* change the product to make it completely your own if you wish, including customizing the content and inserting your own name and brand. And you can pass along the right to resell the product. These are the best, as they support your brand. It's advisable to make edits and include original material, if you can. Other changes should include:

  - Make sure that you use your own affiliate link in the body of the text.

  - Add a footer on every page linking to your website.

  - Repurpose the content. For example, divide up an ebook into articles, compile articles to create an ebook, or create a series of audio or video products out of an ebook.

Digital products – create ebooks or special reports

What is your area of interest or expertise? As we've discussed, a report or ebook will sell if it solves a problem, eases a pain, makes money or saves money. People are willing to pay for solutions. And it doesn't have to be long. In fact, people don't have time to read long books. Just get to the point, make it clear and concise, and your readers will be grateful. Create it in any word processing software such as Microsoft Word, if you have it, or use Open Office for free. Then save it as a .pdf file so it can't be changed after downloading.

✔PDF Tip: Use Neevia Document Converter (http://convert.neevia.com/pdfconvert/) to convert many document formats into PDF - quickly and free. It's an online tool, so no download is necessary. Limit: 1MB per file.

To create a short, usable digital information product, here's an easy way to get started:

1. Go back to the list of problems in your ideal customer profile. Choose one in which you have detailed knowledge or expertise.

2. Ask a friend to sit across the table and listen while you spend 10 minutes talking about the solution to that problem. Have your friend take notes.

3. Use those notes as a guide to write a special report. Make it conversational, just as you did in your talk.

4. State the problem succinctly at the beginning, and then expound on the solution.

5. Use your long tail keywords throughout (3% – or three of every 100 words).

6. Make sure that you use your keywords in the heading, subheads, bullet points and italics.

7. Add a summary at the end.

You now have a great information product that you can sell, give away or publish. This can be the first in a series. Then re-package this information into a video, audio or article. You can expand it to create an e-book. Repeat this process and create 30 more.

Digital products – Create "How-To" videos

Videos are quickly gaining momentum as candy for search engines. Make your video informational, entertaining, short (no more than three minutes) and professional. Use a simple video camera with good audio quality, like Cisco's Flip Video ($199). Explain or demonstrate the steps as a tutorial. Search engines love tutorial videos and people do, too, IF they are packed with informative tips and truly helpful insights. If you just slap it together, junk videos will actually hurt your reputation, so don't waste your time. Create quality, and people will send their friends the link. Spend time doing it right. Viral video will make your traffic soar.

Chapter Eight Highlights

- The Internet offers volumes of digital information that you can purchase very inexpensively and obtain rights to resell from your site.

- It's important to understand the difference between *RR, MRR, and PLR,* as they enable you, as a retailer, to do different things.

- PLR rights are the best, as they are customizable, can be resold and support your brand.

- What is your area of interest or expertise? A short report or ebook will sell if it solves a problem, eases a pain, makes money or saves money.

- When you have a great information product that you can sell, give away or publish, it can be the first in a series. Re-package this information into a video, audio or article. You can expand an article to create an e-book. Repeat this process, and over time, create 30 more.

- Use Neevia Document Converter to convert many document formats into PDF, quickly and free, so others can't change the document.

- Videos are quickly gaining momentum as candy for search engines. Make your video informational, entertaining, short (no more than three minutes) and professional.

- Spend time doing it right – viral video could make your traffic soar.

Chapter Nine

***

Add These to Your Site

Learn the difference between sites that work and sites that don't

In order for your site to be fully functional and effective, these elements are important.

The important call to action

It may sound overly simple, but marketers sometimes get this wrong. They may get so involved in writing about the benefits of the product that they bury the call to action and miss sales. Make sure that the layout of your site includes an obvious and effective call to action element. Your call to action should be:

- Easy for the visitor to see immediately.
- Simple and clear. Tell your visitor *exactly* what you want them to do.
- Easy to take action – one click.

Example: "For 50% off, click here before June 30," designed in large letters, placed toward the top of the page with white space surrounding it – visitors will see it immediately. Your sales will increase because in the moment that they are interested, they know exactly what to do.

Shopping cart capability

Many online entrepreneurs sing the praises of E-junkie. It allows you to sell tangible goods as well as download and sell digital products, including ebooks, MP3 tracks, software, icons, fonts, artwork, phone cards, event tickets, CDs, posters, books, t-shirts, and almost everything else you want to sell.

E-junkie provides shopping cart and buy now buttons, which can be used on your website, blog, landing page, eBay, and Craigslist, among others. E-junkie has no setup fee, no transaction fee and no transaction or bandwidth limits. E-junkie also automates the sales tax, VAT, packaging and shipping costs. It integrates the payment function in a secure area. You can choose from PayPal, Google Checkout, and other pay options. Find E-junkie here: http://www.e-junkie.com

Basic free tools you need for your computer

Your computer may already have these, but double check, and download them if you don't:

Unzip

Many downloaded files are delivered in a "Zip" (compressed) format. In order to unzip them, download a free utility here: http://www.7-zip.org/

View PDF Documents

To view and read PDF documents, download Adobe PDF Reader here: http://get.adobe.com/reader/

View Videos

View videos online with Adobe Flash Player, downloadable here: http://get.adobe.com/flashplayer/

Create videos for free

Create a video slideshow with your own digital pictures, text you create and a video editing program that comes pre-installed on most PCs and Macs. After loading your pictures and text, open the video editing software and follow the instructions in your video editing software. One widely used free software tool enables you to record, save and edit videos - CamStudio (http://camstudio.org/). CamStudio records activity from your screen and audio from a microphone – into AVI video files, and can also convert the AVIs into Streaming Flash Videos (SWFs) using its built-in SWF Producer. It takes some dedication to learn this tool – like most technology.

Make a screen capture video

Use the free version of Jing (http://www.techsmith.com/jing/) to make a screen capture and add an explanatory text box, publish it to Screen-Cast (http://www.Screencast.com), a free hosting site and put the link up on your site. You can load it onto YouTube too, by saving a copy from Jing onto your hard drive.

✔**Free Music Tip:** *Most video programs allow you to imbed music, but be very careful to use ONLY public domain music content in order to avoid a potentially costly copyright infringement lawsuit! Royalty-free music is available free (donations accepted) at Incompetech (www.incompetech.com/m/c/royalty-free/) and sound effects are available free at AudioMicro http://www.audiomicro.com*

Chapter Nine Highlights

- Make sure that the layout of your site includes an obvious and effective *call to action* element. Tell your visitor *exactly* what you want them to do.

- Many online entrepreneurs sing the praises of E-junkie. It allows you to sell tangible goods, as well as download and sell digital products.

- CamStudio is a widely used *free* software tool that enables you to record, save and edit videos.

- Most video programs allow you to imbed music, but be very careful to use *only* your own original music or public domain music content, in order to avoid a potentially costly copyright infringement lawsuit!

Chapter Ten

***

Build Your Prospect List

"Opt-ins": The right way to build lists that convert to paying customers

Your email list is one of the pillars of a solid Internet business. It's *your own* community – people who are highly interested in your niche, the information you offer and your products. Building this highly-targeted list and using it effectively is a core success strategy.

The quality and size of your list could make the difference between long-term success and failure. But you don't want just any list. You want a list that:

- Opted-in to receive your information.

- Is highly interested in your niche – not borrowed from someone else.

- Is fresh and accurate – not old or out of date.

"Opt-in" means that your visitor has entered (at least) their name and email address into an opt-in box on your site, giving you permission to contact them – usually in response to an offer you made, such as a free report. If you don't have opt-in permission, and you contact them anyway, it's considered spam, which you want to avoid completely. Never contact people by email without their permission.

The very best way to ensure the quality of your opt-in email list is to build it yourself.

How to build your email database

Perhaps you already have an email list. Ask yourself: "Is it relevant to my chosen niche? Do the people on this list really care about my niche content and products?" If not, it may be best to start a new list.

You can choose from among many different ways to publish information and promote your site in order to build your opt-in email list, including publish online articles, videos, podcasts, ebooks, reports and engage in social media, to name a few. I delve into these tactics in greater detail in the following pages. For now, we'll focus on how to build your site to capture the traffic that comes your way.

Set up simple landing pages

A landing page, also known as a "squeeze page," is a simple site that has one purpose – to move your prospective customer to click through and purchase. It is becoming the gold standard for converting traffic into paying customers. The simplest are one page, though some have a sales page and a second purchase page. The simpler the better, as Internet users increasingly want instant gratification. The fewer clicks required to get to the meat, the more you will "convert."

Click-through rates vary widely. With repeated testing, tracking and tweaking, you can increase rates as you learn what works best. If you reach 5-10% click-through, by Internet standards, you're doing very well.

The landing page should focus on a really compelling free offer. The more valuable the offer, the more people will click through. For example, offer an ebook packed with useful How-To information, a guide or workbook. Even though you may be able to charge for this information, it will return its value to you again and again, as you make future repeated sales to these email opt-in subscribers. Not only that, but if you offer something they would otherwise be willing to buy, then you instantly gain a reputation for giving great value and they're very likely to pass it on to their friends. Now *that's* a double win for you.

Tips for your landing page

If you design your own landing pages, a few specific elements will greatly enhance their effectiveness and conversion rates:

- Create a compelling headline that captures their attention immediately and intrigues them to read further.

- Be genuine. Too much hype is off-putting.

- Use bullet points to highlight the benefits to your customer.

- Declare a specific *"Call to Action"* – tell them exactly what you want them to do. (Example: "Sign in now to receive your free report.")

- Use arrows to direct their eye to the opt-in box

where they enter their name and email address.

- Place the opt-in box high enough on the page so that your visitor doesn't have to scroll down to find it.

- At the opt-in box, assure them that you will *not* spam or sell their contact information to anyone – ever.

- Keep it simple. Avoid clutter. Make the page appealing to the eye and easy to follow.

Free landing pages

It's enormously fun to find real value – just like you're about to create and offer to your traffic. Here's an example that will drive home this concept. I am about to share with you a site that offers free landing pages, in both video and text formats. See how viral their value offer is? I'm including it in a book! Now your challenge is to come up with a value offer to your niche audience that's really viral. In the meantime, here's the link to the free landing pages (called 'squeeze pages' here): http://www.pluginsqueezepage.com/

✔*Wordpress Tip:* *Special landing page templates are designed to integrate into the theme of your WordPress blog. They are not free, but a great landing page that 'converts' is an investment that returns many times over. "These templates allow you to use your favorite Wordpress theme for your overall website look and feel, while creating individual pages with a different look and feel. These templates are perfect for special offers, affiliate promotions, joint venture offers, email signup pages, squeeze pages, product sales letters, etc." – Jason Keith, Creator (Find it here: http://wp-landingpages.com)*

Where to host your landing page

Landing pages are often hosted with their own unique domain name. This strategy helps your SEO and promotion efforts when you choose a domain name that includes your best long tail keywords. Long domain names are OK for this purpose because keywords in the name are more important than a short name that people will remember. For instance, the domain name for this book, and additional resources, is its title, http://www.thewebpoweredentrepreneur.com   Although I have a complete website there, it could be the site for only a landing page. Buying a domain name and hosting should cost less than $100 a year, but you can also take advantage of free options.

Free hosting

Sites that have the capability to host landing pages for free include WordPress.com and Weebly.com (recommended by *Time* magazine). Both sites have tutorials and resources to help you learn how to use them. I also recommend searching YouTube.com for instructional videos. The most popular tutorial videos on YouTube are those with the most views.

You need an autoresponder

When traffic lands on your site, blog or landing page, you need an opt-in box with an autoresponder. Autoresponders tools that capture your visitors' email addresses and automatically reply with a sequence of follow up emails that you have customized. Your follow up emails must give real value and compel them to take action.

The number of automatic reply emails, the subject lines and the messages in the emails will determine how many people on your list:

- Delete the emails without looking at them.
- Unsubscribe.
- Click through.
- Click through and *convert* – meaning *buy*.

Use an autoresponder system that tracks all these actions and reports them in a way that gives you meaningful information. You want to tweak your messages in order to eventually increase the click-throughs and the conversions/buyers.

Simplify the process

One great autoresponder tool that offers a free startup package (limited to 500 email addresses and 3,000 emails per month) is MailChimp (http://www.MailChimp.com). After you reach those maximums, you can upgrade to their paid level. This tool is widely recognized as a leader in the field, used by corporations such as Intel, Canon, Staples, Vera Wang and others. Additionally, MailChimp offers integration into Wordpress, Twitter, SalesForce.com and other tools that help you automate the entire system.

> ✔*Autoresponder Tip:* *Anticipating that you will very quickly surpass 500 email subscribers, one widely acclaimed tool to use for the long run is Aweber. You can try it for $1 for the first month. After that, pricing is based on the size of your email list – quite affordable, really, given its features and functionality. Aweber is a complete system for creating and managing your email campaigns. They offer email marketing training – webinars, videos and more; plus live, toll-free customer support six days a week. Check it out here: http://www.aweber.com/*

What is the automated follow-up email sequence?

You customize the frequency and content of your follow up email messages. The first one should come instantly upon their opt-in; don't make them wait. First, thank them and then deliver access to what you promised – the free report, or whatever. It could also give more tips, insights or interesting resources. You can't lose by over-delivering. Make "over-delivering" one of your business' core values in order to outshine your competition.

Subsequent follow up emails should deliver even more value. The best type of value is something they can put to work and get results almost immediately, like the free landing pages I mentioned earlier. When you do this, people will welcome your emails and you'll gain a reputation for quality. Your subscribers will tend to stay with you, instead of opting out. Offer unadvertised bonuses, with no hooks or tricks which compromise the trust you're working so hard to build.

Ask for specific feedback and provide a link for them to access others' comments about it. Perhaps you've posted to your blog on the topic, and your subscribers can add their two cents. Many times, the comments are better than the original content. Even *you* will learn from your subscribers. Consider getting stories about how your freebie or product worked for someone and highlight their story (with their permission, of course).

In the process of delivering value, link to one or two of your products, perhaps adding a P.S. like a trusted friend would mention in conversation. But just focus on the value to the reader. If they're interested, they'll click. If they like it enough, they'll buy.

Don't make this list-building mistake

Your follow up emails are not permission to slam them with one-way push promotion messages. If you do this, I promise that you will lose subscribers and your hard-earned reputation for delivering informative, valuable content.

Click-through and conversion rates

For your business to be successful, a certain percentage of your traffic must continue to click through and engage in your sequence, until they take the final call to action – and make the purchase. The *percent* that purchase is called the *conversion rate,* a very important rate to track and continually improve.

The average click-through rate (the percent that click on the call to action link) for an effective email is excellent at 5-10%. Conversion rates vary widely based on the effectiveness of the sales page, call to action, product appeal, etc. Many products claim conversion rates of 2-5%. To project sales, use the click-through rate and the conversion rate.

Let's say that you're selling an affiliate product priced at $198 and they pay 50% commission on each sale, or $99. If you send a mailing to your opt-in subscriber base of 3,000 and experience a click-through rate of 10% and a conversion rate of 3%, you will sell 9 units and earn $445.50 (3,000 x .10 x .03 x $99 x .5 = $445.50).

As you can see, the larger your list, the more money you make!

Increase conversions

With some email and conversion rate experience, you want to focus on increasing both the size of your mailing list (keep it high quality!)

and the conversion rate on the promotional mailing. Internet market-ers with years of trial-and-error experience offer best practice tips for increasing the conversion rate:

- Use only one powerful call to action. If you have multiple items to sell, include those carefully in your follow up or in another campaign. Keep your audience interested in just one thing.

- Make the call to action crystal clear. Keep it simple and make it stand out.

- Place the call to action high enough in the content so that viewers will see it without scrolling down.

- List the benefits in a compelling way. Convey the urgency in buying today. That could be a discount or free bonus.

Since this step is so important, you may wish to test different ver-sions and compare click-through and conversion rates. Keep tweaking to improve your sales.

Chapter Ten Highlights

- Your email list is one of the pillars of a solid Internet business. You're *your own* community – people who are highly interested in your niche, the information you offer and your products. Building this highly-targeted list and using it effectively is a core success strategy.

- "Opt-in" means that your visitor has entered (at least) their name and email address into an opt-in box on your site, giving you permission to contact them.

- A landing page, also known as a "squeeze page," is a simple site that has one purpose – to move your prospective customer to click through and purchase. It is becoming the gold standard for converting traffic into paying customers.

- The landing page should focus on a really compelling *free* offer. The more valuable the offer, the more people will click through.

- Landing pages are often hosted with their own unique domain name. This strategy helps your SEO and promotion efforts when you choose a domain name that includes your best long tail keywords.

- When traffic lands on your site, blog, or landing page, you need an opt-in box with an autoresponder. Autoresponders are tools that capture those email addresses and automatically reply with a sequence of follow up emails that you customized.

- Your follow up emails must give real value and compel them to take action.

- Tweak your messages to continually increase the click-throughs and the conversions/buyers.

- Your follow up emails are not permission to slam them with one-way push promotion messages.

Chapter Eleven

***

Legal Housekeeping for your Home Base Site

Easy and inexpensive legal forms that your website needs

"Transparency" is a value embraced by social media, as well as high integrity Internet business owners, visitors, and customers. Transparent content means WYSIWYG – "What You See Is What You Get." As an online merchant, you want to practice full disclosure in order to build trust and enhance sales.

One important way to be on the up and up: tell your visitors that you have affiliate relationships in place to sell products. Take care of your legal housekeeping. Be sure that you understand your legal responsibilities. Use professional legal notices that are up-to-date and prepared by Internet-experienced legal counsel.

Post website legal compliance notices

On December 1, 2009, the FTC (U.S. Federal Trade Commission) revised its "Guides Concerning the Use of Endorsements and Testimonials in Advertising" that affects most Internet and affiliate marketers. The guides are meant to protect the consumer and require disclosure of for-profit relationships. Contact your own Internet-experienced legal counsel, or consider the packages available online.

Download a free special report by attorney Mike Young entitled, "How to Comply with the New FTC Compensation Disclosure Guidelines" here:

http://mikeyounglaw.com/ftc-disclosure-special-report.pdf

This free report will give you up-to-date knowledge about what to do to stay out of trouble with the FTC. As Mr. Young notes, "Although not a replacement for legal advice from your Internet lawyer, this guide is a better alternative to reading non-lawyers' guesses in forums as to what the FTC is actually doing and how it can affect your online business."

What legal forms does your website need?

According to Internet lawyer Young, "Depending on your business and website, you will probably need from four to ten legal forms for your website to provide basic protection from most legal assaults. When you use the Website Legal Forms Generator™ software, it generates 10 of the most commonly-needed website legal documents." You can review his package here: http://legalformsgenerator.com/

Another option to explore is attorney Jack Campitelli's Internet Law Compliance Guide and forms.

"Internet Law Compliance is the One-Stop-Shop Handbook website operators need to understand and comply with the regulations and requirements for lawfully doing business on the Internet. Complete with forms and disclaimers." – Jack Campitelli, JD

See the features and benefits of this one-stop legal resource here: http://www.internetlawcompliance.com

Chapter Eleven Highlights

- "Transparency" is a value embraced by social media, as well as high integrity Internet business owners, visitors, and customers. Transparent content means WYSIWYG – "What You See Is What You Get." As an online merchant, you want to practice full disclosure in order to build trust and enhance sales.

- Be sure that you understand your legal responsibilities. Use professional legal notices that are up-to-date and prepared by Internet-experienced legal counsel.

- According to Internet lawyer Mike Young, "Depending on your business and website, you will probably need from four to ten legal forms for your website to provide basic protection from most legal assaults."

- Guides and legal forms software are available, affordable, and helpful.

Chapter Twelve

***

Plan to Drive Traffic to Your Site

Craft a promotion plan that grabs attention

Marketing and promotion systems are plastered all over the Internet, claiming to have instant traffic and automatic businesses resulting in explosive profits. Truly successful Internet entrepreneurs will level with you and tell you that there are many effective systems and you can create profitable businesses, but *nothing* is effortless or instantaneous. Just like offline businesses, it requires a strategic, proven plan and focused, consistent work. So create a plan and just get started – one day at a time.

The pages that follow walk you through many types of promotions that work. Choose a few methods that fit your business and make sense to you. Choose things you enjoy. For example, if you don't enjoy writing but you love to perform, then make videos instead of writing articles.

Schedule promotion activities every day. Make it a priority and be consistent. It would be such a shame to get this far, then not cross the finish line! The last chapter of this book lists suggested daily activities to promote your site, and engage your ideal customer.

As you will learn, social media can play a big part in your plan. The exciting thing is, you're already way ahead of the curve. Most people are just playing with social media and don't have an inkling of its power in business promotion.

Backlinks – the key to SEO

Backlinks are links from other sites that are directed to your site. Backlinks are widely regarded as one of the primary building blocks of SEO – important for high ranking by search engines. Google, for instance, gives more credit to sites that have a high number of relevant, high-quality backlinks because Google believes that is an indication of the site's importance.

How do you get high quality, relevant backlinks?

Important: Many of the promotional tactics below involve posting meaningful, keyword-rich content on the Internet. This is the critical strategy you *must* implement in order to drive interested traffic to your site – your ideal customer. This method is called "organic," and is the backbone of search engine optimization.

Choose only high-ranking sites. Page rank is Google's way of assigning a relative importance indicator to a site, for the purpose of its search algorithm. Post *only* relevant material. Your content should *always* include a link back to your site. If you use automated tools and receive irrelevant, low-ranking backlinks, search engines will actually penalize your site for it. There is *no* shortcut method that is automatic, instant, or any other easy way to gain permanent, niche-targeted traffic that yields recurring buyers.

Avoid these link-building strategies

They're called "black hat" techniques, and search engines will penalize you. Stay away from them:

- "Link farms".
- Inter-linking (exchanging links from sites with the same owner).
- Sites that "rank" less than four.
- Purchasing links.
- Sites that engage in illegal activity.

Concentrate on getting highly ranked, relevant, natural backlinks. Place your links only on sites with a page rank of at least four. Five + is better. To quickly determine if a site ranks well enough to warrant your time and your link, use this free Page Rank Checker tool: http://www.prchecker.info/

One important ratio to track is the ratio of inbound to outbound links. You want to have more links point to your site (inbound) than links on your site pointing elsewhere (outbound). Periodically check the number and source of backlinks (inbound) to your site by using this free tool: http://www.backlinkwatch.com/ and then count the links in your site. Calculate inbound/outbound. The answer should be greater than one. Example: 202 inbound / 37 outbound = 5.45 - Good!

✔**Backlink Tip:** *Webconf's free tool offers you a natural way to find relevant sites that invite link requests. Enter your long tail keyword. The result is a list of websites that include the keyword and "Add link," "Add site," "Add URL," "Add website," etc. You can check their page rank, contact the sites you like and request to add your link. This takes time, but quality backlinks are essential to achieve recognition by search engines. Try to do a few each day.* http://www.webconfs.com/backlink-builder.php

Craft headlines to grab attention

As the sheer volume and speed of new Internet content escalates, so does the importance of your headline. I regularly scan my favorite feeds for items that deserve my time. We all do. Those that actually get my attention are those with headlines that pop and promise benefits. There is no cast-in-stone recipe for creating attention-grabbing headlines, but these tips will help:

- Choose your keywords for the content and designate one of them to be used in the headline.

- Designate another one for the subhead.

- Pay attention to others' articles and headlines. Write down headlines that grab your attention and emulate them for your own.

- Promise a benefit.

- Engage the readers' emotions.

- Use hot-off-the-press news topics.

- Make it provocative, creative, edgy or a bit startling.

- Tie in to a highly trafficked celebrity. For example: "7 Basics Simon Cowell Should Know About Social Engagement."

✔*Content Tip:* How to get attention. According to Justin Osofsky, Facebook's Developer Blog Manager, "In our analysis of stories published by top media organizations, we found that (a) stories involving emotional topics, passionate debates, and important sports events have 2-3x the activity of other stories, (b) status updates which ask simple questions or encourage a user to Like the story have 2-3x the activity, and (c) stories published in the early morning or just before bedtime have higher engagement."

A word about social media's unique culture

Before you plunge into devising your social media promotion strategy and using social media tools, let's take a moment to establish the framework of excellence that is utilized in social media. It involves a culture of:

- Authenticity – Be real; be yourself. Social media is about real people, real relationships and trust building.

- Transparency – Disclose truth, don't hide anything and don't use tricks.

- Giving value – Offer meaningful, useful information. People appreciate that and will come back.

- Building naturally – This takes time, but it's worth it. Online tools can help automate some processes, but nothing is instant - no matter what tremendous claims you read online.

- Opting in – Invite others to seek more information about you. Don't spam. (According to Wikipedia: "Spam is the use of electronic messaging systems – including most broadcast media, digital delivery systems – to send unsolicited messages indiscriminately.") Spam is *bad*.

Chapter Twelve Highlights

- Truly successful Internet entrepreneurs will level with you and tell you that there are many effective systems and you can create profitable businesses, but NOTHING is effortless or instantaneous.

- Schedule some promotion activities every day. Make it a priority and be consistent.

- Backlinks are widely regarded as one of the primary building blocks of SEO – very important for high ranking by search engines.

- Many of the most successful promotional tactics involve posting meaningful, keyword-rich content on the Internet. This is the critical strategy you *must* implement in order to drive highly interested traffic to your site – your ideal customer.

- There is no shortcut method that is automatic, instant, or any other easy way to gain permanent, niche-targeted traffic that yields recurring buyers.

- As the sheer volume and speed of new content escalates, the importance of your headline does, too.

Those that actually get a busy reader's attention have headlines that pop and promise benefits.

- Social media's unique culture is grounded in the tenets of:
  - ° Authenticity.
  - ° Giving value.
  - ° Opting in.
  - ° Building naturally.

Chapter Thirteen

***

Start to Drive Traffic to Your Site

Ten strategic and successful ways to begin – free

We love free. These 10 online marketing tactics are the basics. Once you accomplish momentum with these, then spend time every day to try more tactics and dig further into your marketing toolbox. Attract traffic for free:

1. Pay special attention to your site's search engine optimization. Review your SEO activities and make sure that your keywords attract the niche traffic and ideal customer you target.

2. Submit your site to search engines and major indexes.

3. Add fresh content to your site frequently. Search engines crawl your site regularly and they LOVE fresh content.

4. Concentrate on getting natural links from high

page rank, "dofollow" sites in your niche. (More on dofollow later). Only the first link pointing to a site counts.

5. Get traffic from social bookmarking sites.

6. Use AddThis.com to make it easy for others to bookmark your site, which is best.

7. Build your friends and fans following on social media sites.

8. Include keywords and links to your site and social media profiles in everything you post.

9. Add your site link and social media links to your email signature.

10. Include your site and social media links in all off-line promotions.

Use these strategies to build more traffic

Interesting, keyword-rich content, posted around the Internet, and linking to your site will create consistent, laser-targeted traffic. Use these strategies in a thoughtful plan that suits your business niche and ideal customer. Choose a few to start. Commit time every day – slow and steady wins the race. Use a few tools to help automate the process, or outsource, if you have the budget. Commit to building your traffic and convert them into customers.

Submit your site to search engines

Do this first. You'll cover the most ground with this one tactic. Search engines need to know you exist, and if you wait for them to find you, it may take months.

The first site that really matters is Google, followed by Yahoo! and Bing. As we mentioned earlier, they collectively represent about 95% of search activity online. So, submit to these three, because any time spent submitting to others yields dramatically diminishing returns. For now, focus on:

Google

If you're new to sharing your content with Google, here's how to get started:

1. Submit your domain name/URL for inclusion in Google's index. It does not require account setup: http://www.google.com/addurl/?continue=/addurl

2. Submit a Sitemap through Webmaster Tools: http://www.google.com/webmasters/tools/

3. List your business in Google Places: http://www.Google.com/places

Yahoo!

Yahoo! offers a free search submit, as well as a directory submit that requires payment. At a minimum, submit your site to the free search which requires you to set up an account:

- Yahoo! search submit (free): http://siteexplorer.search.yahoo.com/submit

- Yahoo! directory submit (paid): https://ecom.yahoo.com/dir/submit/intro/

Bing

Submitting your site is easy – it does not require account setup: http://www.bing.com/webmaster/SubmitSitePage.aspx

Submit your site to Open Directory Project

The Open Directory Project (ODP) is maintained by live expert editors and all submissions must pass their evaluation. While it is well worth the time to manually submit to ODP, you must first understand their policies in order to avoid rejection.

Submit to Open Directory Project: http://www.dmoz.org/add.html

✔ **Submission Tip:** *If you want to go the extra mile and spend $97 to have your site submitted to virtually every (over 2000) quality search engines, directories and classified sites, then try Submit Equalizer. Submit Equalizer is PC software that is easy to download and run on your computer. And you can re-submit your sites as much as you want, because you own the software: http://www.submitequalizer.com*

AddThis

AddThis is a free tool that helps website owners/publishers and bloggers spread their content across the web by making it easy for visitors to bookmark and share content with their friends and favorite social destinations such as: Facebook, Twitter, MySpace, StumbleUpon and Digg. It also enables visitors to print or email a page. AddThis can be used to share just about anything, including:

- Websites.

- Blogs.

- Email newsletters.

- MySpace profiles.

- Microsoft Office Live workspaces.

- Flash websites and widgets.

- Other embedded content.

It's easy to install. Decide where on your site or content you want to place the button. Go to the AddThis website and create your code by clicking "Get Your Button." If you want analytics, you must create an account. Next, just copy and paste the HTML code where you want the button. AddThis offers more detailed information on their FAQ page: http://www.addthis.com/help/faq

Write like a news professional

This point cannot be over-emphasized. When you write content for ebooks, articles, comments and tweets, hype is considered spam or trash. You can, and often WILL, be blocked for using a highly-promotional writing style.

So what do you do? Write like a news professional. Give solid information instead of opinions. Offer reviews, with pros and cons, but not hype.

Consider these two statements. Which one is opinionated?

1. ULTRA-PURE HAWAII WATER® is the best of Hawaii and the finest in the world.

2. ULTRA-PURE HAWAII WATER'S® source is a virgin rain forest that naturally filters down for 25 years to collect in the Halawa Aquifer.

Write about user benefits, too. Readers love to discover what something will do for them – how it will help them. That's the kind of content that gets shared and could go viral.

Why is "dofollow" important?

One often overlooked aspect of posting comments for backlinks is the concept of "dofollow" (vs. 'nofollow'). When you post content or comments in order to gain traffic to your site, nofollow sites do not give you search engine ranking credit for the link. While links on nofollow sites DO allow visitors to click through to your site, they do *not* add to your SEO efforts to increase your standing with search engines.

So if you're trying to increase *both* visitor traffic and search engine ranking, post comments on sites that dofollow. I *highly* recommend that you spend at least a portion of your valuable link-building time on dofollow sites. Here is an excellent article, "How to Determine if a Website Offers Dofollow or Nofollow Links":

http://www.ehow.com/how_4880498_website-offers-follow-nofollow-links.html

Post on community forums & blogs

Get recognition in your niche and invite targeted traffic to your site by commenting on blogs, forums, and social media groups. Spend time each day doing this, and you will also establish valuable backlinks that help your search engine ranking. Answer questions or make meaningful comments on subjects that are relevant to your subject matter.

Include your keywords in the text, and your name with your link at the end. Try posting on these sites:

- Ehow http://www.ehow.com/
- Yahoo! Answers http://answers.yahoo.com/
- WikiAnswers http://wiki.answers.com/
- WikiHow http://www.wikihow.com/

As a Subject Matter Expert, it's important that you find places that are relevant to your business. Those could be niche-specific:

- Groups on http://www.Facebook.com, http://www.LinkedIn.com or http://www.Groups.Google.com - or others you find by search.
- Community FORUMS you find by searching Google for "(topic) forum".
- Blogs that focus on your niche. Also search Google "(topic) blog."

One expert has compiled and published a list of dofollow blogs: "The Ultimate Dofollow Blog List with High Page Rank": http://niceblogger.com/2009/08/21/dofollow-list/

An SEO expert offers this "List of 150 PR 1-8 Dofollow Forums": http://atniz.com/2010/10/18/list-of-150-pr1-8-dofollow-forums/

✔**Dofollow Blog Tip:** *Try this dofollow search engine that has indexed over 170,000 pages of dofollow blogs, with Page Rank between two and seven. Sign up for a two-day free trial: http://dofollowsearchengine.com/ Or find more dofollow search engines here:*

http://www.maskuncoro.net/top-5-dofollow-search-engine

Listen to the conversation first. Get a feel for the tone and topics of interest. Then, after you're familiar with the audience and their conversation, start to comment on others' posts, or answer questions. In this way, you begin to establish your reputation as a subject matter expert. More tips for engaging:

- Make sure that what you post is timely, relevant, and meaningful.

- Add real value to the conversation.

- *Use your keywords.* This is content that will be crawled and found by search engines.

- Ask questions of others.

- *Do not* use promotional language. This is not where you advertise yourself, your products, or your business.

- You may use a business title after your name and a link to your website. People will click through to learn more about you *if* you add value.

- Occasionally, you may announce an event or make an offer of value to the audience. (Something free is always good.)

Most importantly, listen, learn, be inspired, and have fun! This is *social*.

✔**Blog Comment Submission Tip:** *"SEO Blog Submitter is an application that allows you to perform searches among blogs powered by popular blog platforms (Wordpress, Drupal, etc.) according to user-defined keywords. The application not only bares blog pages, but also analyzes the content and retrieves specific criteria, allowing you to pick blog pages suitable for SEO needs. For example: all dofollow pages with PR>3, containing more than 10 comments with no need to register for commenting. After selecting blog pages, you can open them in the integrated browser and submit comments either manually or using built-in Auto Fill feature." Not free, but a time saver for quality backlinks: http://seodevgroup.com/products/seoblogsubmitter.html*

Write articles

Start by writing articles that capture the attention of your niche audience. Go back to the ideal customer profile you created earlier. The topics of your articles will come from those lists – their problems, needs and interests. Articles get attention and help your sales when they:

- Use laser-targeted keywords. Use them in the heading, subheads, and italicize and bold them.

- Start with attention-grabbing headlines. Do a bit of Google research on "How to create article headlines that sell."

- Give real instructional value – insights, tips, how-to information. That's what people search for.

- Are worthy of passing on to friends with similar interests. Make it "viral".

- Contain links to your site and products.

- Are about 300 words in length – 400 *max*.

- End with a compelling call to action. Tell your visitor *exactly* what you want them to do, "Click here now."

Since Google loves new content, articles are the perfect way to offer your ideal customers real value. Don't scrimp on giving valuable information. Internet businesses are fast becoming proficient at it, and the quality of free information is escalating every day.

Over a short time period, write 30 meaningful articles that direct visitors to your site. Your articles should be very informative and help the reader solve a problem, ease a pain, make money, save money, or otherwise give great insights and value. When your article entices them to learn more, they *will* click on the link that takes them to your landing page. Post these articles over a reasonable length of time. Don't flood the market with them all at once (2-3 per week is okay).

Headlines are enormously important. Like it or not, attention-grabbing headlines and effective copy online are evolving into a somewhat formulaic art form:

- Make a promise (and deliver).

- Keep it short.

- Use a keyword.

Here are some examples of *great headlines*. You may find them a bit cheesy, but it's been proven time and again that *they work*:

- Your Must-Know Guide to _____
- Make More Money With _____
- 5 Steps to Reduce Your _____ Costs
- 7 Questions You Must Ask For _____

Promote your articles by submitting them to article directories. According to Wikipedia, "Article directories are a form of Search Engine Optimization where companies and professional writers submit articles based on a specific niche." The top five article directories by page rank, are:

1. EzineArticles www.ezinearticles.com

2. ArticlesBase www.articlesbase.com

3. Suite 101 www.suite101.com

4. Buzzle www.buzzle.com

5. Helium www.helium.com

Dofollow Article Directory list:
http://dofollow.info/dofollow-article-directories/

✔*Article Submission Tip:* Instant Article Submitter is PC software THAT you can run right on your computer. It submits to the major directories (most with high page-rank) so you get maximum exposure without having to labor for days on end. Not Free, is certainly a time saver: http://www.instantarticlesubmitter.com/indexmr.html

✔*Link Tip:* Include your articles' links on social media sites. Use them naturally when you create your profile, post or update. Give the audience a reason to click through, such as, "I just published an awesome list (place link here) of 10 ways to save big on school supplies – like searching 'school supplies coupon code.'" This is 116 characters (without the link) and can be tweeted – and retweeted (more on that later.)

Issue press releases

Press releases are a great way to get content and links out on the Internet quickly. Let people know about anything truly newsworthy. The launch of your business is newsworthy. The addition of a new product is newsworthy. Hitting business milestones, new business partners, and conducting events are all legitimate news for press releases.

Generally, cover who, what, when, where and why. Write about 350-375 words and:

- Grab attention in the title (using a keyword!) with something new or catchy.

- Use a subtitle.

- Tell a great story with human interest.

- Quote someone.

- Use links for more information.

In news releases optimized for the Internet, add social media features that enable readers to find it, save it and pass it on:

- Use your keywords throughout.

- Enable comments and trackbacks (if using a service such as PRWeb.com).

- Include an RSS feed for folks to subscribe.

- Add a button for readers to submit it to Digg or Delicious.

- Tag it with Technorati to make it easy to find.

(More on these later, too.)

Submit your press releases widely to free PR sites with relatively high ranking, as listed at PRSiteList.com (http://prsitelist.com/):

http://www.prlog.org/
http://www.24-7pressrelease.com/
http://www.1888pressrelease.com/
http://www.pr-inside.com/
http://www.onlineprnews.com/

http://www.beforeitsnews.com/

http://www.pressreleasepoint.com/

http://www.i-newswire.com/

http://www.release-news.com/

http://www.//bignews.biz/

http://www.newswiretoday.com/index.php

http://www.pr-usa.net/

http://www.openpr.com/

http://www.clickpress.com/releases/

http://www.booshplr.com/

http://www.pressbox.co.uk/index.html

http://www.pressabout.com/

http://www.SANEPR.com/

Access "25 Free Dofollow Press Release Sites":

http://www.youngprepro.com/uncategorized/25-free-dofollow-press-release-sites/

✔**Press Release Tip:** *Since you can achieve a lot of backlinks in a very short time by submitting press releases, many folks use software called Press Equalizer. Like many automation tools, it costs $97, so you have to decide if the time saving benefit is worth the cost – for you and your marketing strategy. http://www.pressequalizer.com/*

Distribute videos

It's not necessary to produce a studio-quality video. Any inexpensive camcorder, even your cell phone, can work well *provided* that it has great content and acceptable sound quality. No one wants to strain to hear you, which just hurts your reputation and cheapens your brand. Make sure the sound quality is good.

Post your video free on YouTube (http://www.YouTube.com) and be sure to use your keywords. Place your chosen keywords in the title and anchor text. Place a link to your site on your profile page. Enable visitors to imbed your video. A significant number of visitors are there to grab the imbed link for their blog, article or content. They also tweet about it. Many video hosting sites make social media integration easier. Take advantage of these features, which are explained on their site.

In addition to YouTube, you can also load it onto other top video sites:

1. Vimeo http://www.vimeo.com

2. MetaCafe http://www.metacafe.com

3. Hulu http://www.hulu.com

4. Veoh http://www.veoh.com

5. Video Google http://video.google.com/

6. Yahoo! Video http://www.video.yahoo.com

7. Blip http://www.blip.tv

Access "12 'Dofollow' Video Sharing Sites to Distribute Videos and Build Links":

http://www.searchenginejournal.com/dofollow-video-sharing-sites/8763/

Online services are increasingly making your video distribution job easier! One such service offers a free version – Tube Mogul (http://www.tubemogul.com). It will distribute your uploaded video to the top video hosting and social media platforms. Upload your video once (using the OneLoad option), and it can also be deployed to custom sites. It will create an RSS feed to syndicate your video anywhere. Tube Mogul provides analytics so that you can track viewings – who, when and where.

Post the link to your video or imbed the video itself into your website, blog or landing page.

Send an email to everyone on your list – with a link to your video (and tell them why it's worth their time to watch it!)

✔*Video Tip:* *One new tool makes video distribution a snap. They automate the process and help you achieve high Google ranking for your long tail keywords. TrafficGeyser.com charges for this service, but they do offer a free trial. If video is one of your primary marketing strategies, then it may be worth the monthly fee to save you time and escalate your search engine rankings. Watch the demonstration video on their site:http://www.trafficgeyser.com/*

How do you make videos go viral?

How do you create viral videos? That's the million-dollar question! Some experts study this in depth and agree on a few key concepts:

- Create intense emotional impact. (Think puppies, children, car crashes, laughing out loud.)

- Create a sense of HOPE, inspiration, or promise.

- Create something unexpected – give it a surprising, ironic or humorous twist.

- People like to share good news.

Get creative!

Record and post podcasts

Podcasting is like radio on demand. To learn how to create a podcast, and much, much more, visit Podcasting-tools (http://podcasting-tools.com) "...a comprehensive podcasting resource detailing everything you need to know about Podcasting...Podcasts are designed to include talk shows, tutorials, music, or other audio content." On their home page, click on the link on the upper left, "How to Podcast" for everything you need to know (and then some!) Here's a link to their article, "Make Your First Podcast":

http://www.podcastingnews.com/articles/How-to-Podcast.html

> ✔*Audio Recording Tip:* Audacity (*http://audacity.sourceforge.net/*) is a free, easy-to-use and multilingual audio editor and recorder for Windows, Mac OS X, GNU/Linux and other operating systems. You can use Audacity to:
>
> - Record live audio.
> - Convert tapes and records into digital recordings or CDs.
> - Edit number of different types of sound files.
> - Cut, copy, splice or mix sounds together.
> - Change the speed or pitch of a recording.
> - And more.... See their complete list of features.

Post a link to your podcast, or imbed the podcast itself, into your website, blog or landing page. Add your podcast to a podcast distribution service such as iTunes.com for search engines to find.

Post to classified ad sites

Many Internet marketers swear by online classified ads. The most used site is Craigslist, which sorts by city. This is an appropriate place to use promotional copy, highlighting the benefits of your product. Or, you could offer something of value, direct them to your opt-in landing page, and build your email list.

There is one caveat with classified ad sites. The ads usually expire, so you are not creating a permanent link. Additionally, a dofollow list of classified ad sites is not readily available at this time.

Because spammers love to crawl classified ads for email addresses, you should set up a separate email account (Google's Gmail is free) for all of your ad postings.

- Craigslist http://www.craigslist.org
- Backpage http://www.backpage.com
- Kijiji (owned by Ebay) http://www.kijiji.ca
- USFreeAds http://www.usfreeads.com
- Oodle http://www.oodle.com

For a longer list, search Google for: "List of free classified ad sites."

Write an ebook

The electronic book market is exploding with the advent of the electronic book reader, such as Amazon's Kindle, Sony Reader and Apple iPad. People are eager to load content onto them especially if it's something they enjoy or need. Several websites make publishing an ebook easy:

- Smashwords http://www.smashwords.com
- YouPublish http://www.youpublish.com

At these sites, you can upload your digital content files (ebooks) for free. Then you can give them away, or sell them. Additionally, Lulu (http://www.lulu.com) offers a host of pre-publishing, marketing and distribution services.

Ebooks are an enticing way to get email subscribers to opt-in. Usually free, they offer in-depth information, complemented by links and more resources. In order to implement an e-book strategy effectively, choose one significant problem from your customer profile list and expound upon the solution. Don't cover a range of issues (or opportunities) in an e-book. Rather, make it 15-20 pages and repeat for additional topics. It's not necessary or good business to give everything away in one ebook.

If you're unfamiliar with the format and content of ebooks, search Google for "free ebooks" and take a look at a few of them. Choose one or two that you like as models and just start writing! By laying out the table of contents first, you can narrow your focus and organize your thoughts for writing the content.

Publish an email newsletter

Email newsletters are one of the oldest and most used forms of connecting with your database. They are used so much that most folks avoid them, unless you happen to offer content so amazing that you aren't "unsubscribed" immediately.

Such over-the-top newsletter content takes a great deal of time to gather and write. Then there's the task of creating the newsletter regularly. Some niches may be more open to newsletters than others, so I advise searching in your niche to find out what's already available. If your competition has captured the niche with their newsletter, seriously consider how you could be different and better. If you can't think of a powerful way to make the audience sit up and take notice, then perhaps your time is better spent on other more rewarding efforts.

If you decide to create a newsletter, here are some important tips:

- Decide on a meaningful slant, such as offering solutions to the audience's most pressing problems.

- Include tips, coupons, profile your readers, links to interesting resources online (such as free webinars or blogs), ask readers questions and solicit feedback, and generally make it really interesting.

- Use your keywords.

- Layout the content so readers know at a glance what they will get out of it.

- Use short, attention-grabbing titles.

- Mix up the content to hold readers' interest.

- Place bullet points at the top of the page to identify the topics covered in the page below.

At the bottom, include your contact information, your logo, and your URL.

✔**Email Newsletter Tip:** *Constant Contact (http://www.constantcontact.com) is an email system that handles much more than just sending emails. They can also conduct online surveys and event registration if you need it. Additionally, they have tutorials for using social media with email and often offer a free 60-day trial.*

Conduct online events – audio and web conferencing

With experience in your niche and all the content you've amassed in the form of ebooks, articles, blog posts; an online event is the perfect way to reach more people who want to learn. Called webinars (online seminars) and teleseminars (phone only), they are exploding now, and so is the technology – to deliver them more easily. Webinars are generally offered to consumers free these days, but can be a great newsworthy event for press releases and email blasts. Webinars and teleseminars are the perfect vehicle to build your email list.

As the host, conduct the event in a natural way – using a friendly, conversational tone. Give real value. Deliver an information-packed seminar so that people will recommend you to others. And when you promote the webinar, ask for questions upfront, so you can be prepared with meaningful answers and resources.

For lots of detailed information on how to run a webinar, visit Best-ForWebinars.com: http://www.bestforwebinars.com

✔*Conferencing Tip:* *ReadyTalk (http://www.readytalk.com) is a very af-fordable alternative to other webinar companies, and offers a variety of functions for conferences of all sizes. They offer audio and web conferencing, recording, and social media tools that publicize upcoming events and share content afterward on Facebook and Twitter.*

Advertise online cost-effectively

Paid online advertising may be a good option for you if you have a marketing budget, proven, productive keywords and need immediate results. Further, it may be a cost-effective choice if you sell a big ticket item and the cost clearly justifies the sales revenue.

Two industry leaders in paid advertising are Google AdWords (http://www.google.com/adwords) and Yahoo! Search Marketing (http://searchmarketing.yahoo.com/en_SG/index.php).

Additionally, you can now advertise on Facebook (http://www.facebook.com/adsmarketing/). Google AdWords offers an extensive learning center – you may pick and choose subjects for your own learning curve:

http://adwords.google.com/support/aw/bin/static.py?hl=en&page=examstudy.cs

Ad campaigns use a pay-per-click (PPC) model (Facebook also offers a cost-per-impressions ad model, or CPM). When people search for your chosen keyword, Google, Yahoo! and Facebook display your ad that contains a link to your site. With PPC, you only pay when someone clicks on your ad. With CPM, you pay per thousand impressions, whether they click or not.

The keywords you choose are critical to the success of your campaign. First, decide how much you're willing to spend on the campaign AND what returns will make that campaign profitable.

Calculate the payback

Start by calculating your conversion ratio: Divide your monthly click-throughs by your monthly sales revenue from those click-throughs. Then, to convert that number into a percentage, simply multiply it by 100. For instance, if you get 10,000 click-throughs and sell 250 products, your conversion ratio is (250/10,000) x 100 = 2.5%. Or, for every 100 click-throughs, you sell 2.5 products.

You charge $125 for the product, so for forecasting purposes, your revenue from that ad should be $125 x 2.5 = $312.50 for every 100 click-throughs.

To determine how much you can bid on a keyword in the campaign, divide your revenue per 100 click-throughs by 100 ($312.50 / 100 = $3.12) and this is your break even bid - $3.12. This is the most you are willing to pay for that keyword, anticipating breaking even. If you paid more, you would anticipate losing money.

When you use longer tail keywords that are less expensive and your click-throughs remain high, your profitability increases. Experiment and tweak the ad, sales page, or call to action to increase the click-throughs, thus further increasing profitability.

Each of the advertising programs works a bit differently and it's quite important to spend time learning the ins and outs before you dive in. If you don't, you could waste a lot of time and money. Each of them offers instruction, but the real tips are often available in forums, articles, or blog posts on specific topics. Search Google for information like, "How does Google AdWords work?" or "How does Yahoo! Search

Marketing work?" for consumers' explanation of their experiences and insider tips.

Create your own Internet radio show

Perhaps you love to talk, rather than write. If so, Internet radio may just be for you! Internet radio sites are the rage, with many offering free hosting for beginner packages. BlogTalkRadio (http://www.blogtalkradio.com) is free, and offers anyone with a computer and telephone access to their system.

On BlogTalkRadio, broadcasters create and share their original content, their voices and their opinions in a public worldwide forum. Visit their site to browse categories. Find your niche. When you become a talk show host, your program can be connected to social media networks such as Facebook, Twitter, and Ning, among others.

Chapter Thirteen Highlights

- Interesting, keyword-rich content posted around the Internet and linking to your site will create consistent, quality traffic.

- Commit some time every day to build traffic – slow and steady wins the race.

- First, submit your site to search engines. They need to know you exist.

- AddThis is a free tool that helps website owners/publishers and bloggers spread their content across the web by making it easy for visitors to bookmark and share your content to their friends and favorite social destinations, such as: Facebook, Twitter,

MySpace, StumbleUpon, and Digg.

- When you write content for ebooks, articles, comments, and tweets, hype is considered spam, i.e. trash. You can – and often *will* – be blocked for using a highly-promotional writing style.

- When you post content or comments in order to gain traffic to your site, nofollow sites do not give you search engine ranking credit for the link. So if you're trying to increase BOTH visitor traffic AND search engine ranking, post comments on sites that dofollow.

- Get recognition in your niche and invite targeted traffic to your site by commenting on blogs, forums, and social media groups.

- Write 30 meaningful articles that direct visitors to your site. Your articles should be very informative and help the reader solve a problem, ease a pain, make money, save money, or otherwise give great insights and value.

- Press Releases are a great way to get content and links out on the Internet quickly.

- Distribute videos. Any inexpensive camcorder, even your phone, can work well *provided* that it has great content and acceptable sound quality.

- Record and post podcasts.

- Post to classified ad sites.

- Write an ebook.

- Publish an email newsletter.

- Advertise online.
- Create your own Internet radio show.

Chapter Fourteen

***

Social Media Overview

Social Media Overview: What you need to know

We've referred to several social media sites, but haven't covered the big picture of the social media landscape. Thousands of sites serve different needs and niche communities. If you're not familiar with the landscape, I suggest that you take a glance at SEOmoz.org's list of the top 101 social media sites here:

http://www.seomoz.org/article/social-media-marketing-tactics#101-social-media-sites

Just as in any industry, different sites specialize in different aspects of social media. They've carved out their own niche. SEOmoz also offers a quick look at the top social media sites *and their niche focus.* SEOmoz's overall top ten are:

1. Facebook.com

2. Twitter.com

3. LinkedIn.com

4.   Wikipedia.com

5.   MySpace.com

6.   Digg.com

7.   YouTube.com

8.   StumbleUpon.com

9.   Reddit.com

10.   Yelp.com

Access SEOmoz's entire list of 25, with descriptions of the sites, links, and more information on each one:

http://www.seomoz.org/article/social-media-marketing-tactics#top-25-social-media-sites

SEOmoz is also a great resource for helpful tools, guides, and services that help businesses grow and prosper. You can access all that here: http://www.seomoz.org

Social media overview

The section below summarizes the categories of social media niches, with a brief overview and examples of top sites.

Social networking

Social networking sites attract people of like-minded interests to add friends, share content, and post messages. In addition to the gigantic general interest sites such as Facebook.com, LinkedIn.com, MySpace.com, Twitter.com, Bebo.com, Friendster.com, Hi5.com, Orkut.com, etc., you want to identify where YOUR ideal niche customers congregate online. Do this by searching Google, "(topic) social networking sites."

Social bookmarking

Social bookmarking sites give users a place to create online access (bookmarks) to their favorite sites and share the content with others. Sites such as Digg.com, Delicious.com, Reddit.com, StumbleUpon.com, etc., are great places to collect your niche-specific sites for later reference when you need to login and post articles, comments, and engage with your ideal customers.

> ✔*Social Bookmarking Tip:* *Social Bookmarking Tip: Clipmarks.com allows you to clip parts of web pages and capture only the most relevant pieces without having to bookmark the entire page.*

Blogs

Blogs are essentially journals that allow anyone to grab their own spot, write and publish online. Blogs and blog posts exist for virtually any topic imaginable. One common and interesting feature is reader comments, which are often just as valuable as the blog content itself. Blog platforms have become very sophisticated and yet user-friendly. Blogs offer options and plugins that transform the simple journal into a site that functions much like a website. Many are free and some require payment. Blogger.com, Tumblr.com, and WordPress.com (the current market leader) are all web-based (no software download necessary) and free.

Wikis

A wiki is a site created to store content added by multiple users from multiple locations at different times. Wikipedia.com is the frontrunner and a preferred source of information on just about anything you can imagine.

Photo sharing

Picassa.com, PhotoBucket.com, Flickr.com, WordPress.com and tinypic.com all allow you to upload and host your digital images for free. From there, you can post them to websites, blog, social media sites – and, well, anywhere.

✔**Photo Sharing Tip:** *If you're into photography, try uploading and* **selling** *your photo rights at these sites: Photostockplus.com, Shutterpoint.com, iStock-photo.com, and Veer.com, among others. They have varied commission and payout programs so read the fine print.*

Video sharing

Upload and share your videos at these top sites: YouTube.com, MetaCafe.com, Vimeo.com, Hulu.com, and Blip.tv. You may designate public or private access and post from this site to others – with a link or imbed directly into content on another site.

Presentation sharing

PowerPoint and similar slideshows offer users the convenience of at-a-glance information with the ability to click through at their own speed. Unlike videos that have limited text, slides can also capture a high volume of your important keywords. Use these top free sites: SlideShare.com, AuthorStream.com, and SlideBoom.com. Content on slide sharing sites is crawled by search engines so include links to your site.

Reviews

The leading review site by far is Yelp.com. Review sites tend to be niche and product-oriented so search Google for "(topic) reviews" to zero in on your ideal customer community. Posting on these sites can attract traffic and add valuable backlinks to your site.

> ✔*Review Tip:* *To get those coveted customer testimonials for use on your site or your social media pages, take a look at Propadoo (http://www.Propadoo.com). They offer a free version and make it easy to get testimonials. Features include: links on your site (easy copy and paste), prewritten email templates (just send them to your customers asking for testimonials), and a feed of testimonials to your site. The testimonials are recognized by search engines, enhancing your brand's online reputation and SEO.*

Social news

Get the latest and most intriguing news from across the globe or in your special niche. Social news sites offer instant access to news and deliver it to you in a plethora of modes (email, feeds, mobile, etc.) These breaking stories are tremendous content topics for your tweet, site content, blog post, article, etc., and are much more likely to be spread to others. You can submit your link, vote, and engage socially. Reddit (http://www.reddit.com) is a source for what's new and popular online. Vote on links that you like or dislike and help decide what's popular, or submit your own.

RSS feed readers (example: http://www.google.com/reader) gather everything on pre-selected sites, but some aggregation sites, like Google News Topix (http://www.topix.com/com/google), rely on software to crawl the Web and spot keywords in news stories. News is continually updated from thousands of sources around the net. Others, like Digg (http://www.digg.com), ask anyone on the Web to suggest stories. Many readers use Twitter as a user-generated newsfeed.

Social publishing

Social publishing sites make it easy for anyone to publish, share, and discover original content. Authors can upload their work and publish keyword-rich content with backlinks to their site. Scribd (http://www.scribd.com) is the largest social publishing and reading site in the world. Squidoo (http://www.squidoo.com) hosts hundreds of thousands of hand-built web pages (which they call "lenses"). Each lens is one person's look at something online. They help build identity, search engine recognition and backlinks on any number of topics of your choice.

Chapter Fourteen Highlights

- Just as in any industry, different sites specialize in different aspects of social media.

- Categories of social media niches include:

  1. Social networking – people of like-minded interests to add friends, share content, and post messages.

  2. Social bookmarking – give users a place to create online access (bookmarks) to their favorite sites, and share content with others.

3. Blogs – journals that allow anyone to grab their own spot, write and publish online.

4. Wikis – sites created to store content added by multiple users from multiple locations at different times.

5. Photo sharing – allows you to upload and host your digital images.

6. Video sharing – upload and share your videos.

7. Presentation sharing – PowerPoint and similar slideshows offer users the convenience of at-a-glance information with the ability to click through at their own speed.

8. Reviews – the public places original reviews of products, sites, content, etc.

9. Social news – instant access to news delivered to you in a plethora of modes (email, feeds, mobile, etc.).

10. Social publishing – makes it easy for anyone to publish, share, and discover original content.

Chapter Fifteen

***

Social Media Marketing Plan

How to plan and build a powerful social media presence and tell your story

In addition to your primary site, social media sites leverage your messages online. The wonder of social media is that it naturally connects people who have similar interests. You want to reach your friends and your friends' friends.

When you engage in discussions online through social media, your message can even "go viral," gaining momentum and reaching well beyond your friend's friends.

The ultimate goal of an Internet marketing campaign is to create a meaningful message that reaches its target audience and is virally spread to others who are interested in the topic.

Build your social media presence and interaction very deliberately. Certain basic fundamentals will make your social media efforts most rewarding:

- Write down your business goals.

- Find and listen to the conversations that are already taking place online about you, your products, your competitors and your competitors' products.

- Find and listen to your ideal customers' needs. Remember, when you offer a solution that solves a pressing problem, fulfills an urgent need, or gives them hope and joy, people will eagerly buy it.

- Choose key social media sites for your target niche and establish your online profile.

- Integrate those sites for maximum exposure, brand-building, and traffic.

- Engage in conversations.

- Build your network or following. Build your email database.

- Track and monitor activity and results.

- Tweak to continually improve results.

- Repeat.

We cover the How-To's in the following pages.

Tell your story – the social media way

You have a unique story to tell, and social media is your opportunity to join conversations. As we discussed earlier, social media is NOT one-way 'push' marketing. It IS about finding online platforms where people have conversations about specific topics of interest and engage in meaningful, two-way discussion.

A site that allows users to interact and add content – comments, links, photos, video, etc. – is social. Use first person. Make your interaction sound and feel genuine. The people you meet online will be attracted to you (and what you offer) when you add helpful, meaningful input. If you're new to social media, it is widely recommended that you first *listen* to the conversation in order to become familiar with its unique style and flow.

Begin by listening – Google Alerts

Sign up for Google Alerts (http://www.google.com/alerts), a free service that searches Google's index, including blogs, news, video, groups and the Internet, for keywords that you specify. Google alerts will automatically send the results to your email inbox or by RSS feed as often as you wish. You might start with:

- Company & product name(s).
- Keywords you determined earlier.
- Competitors' company & product name(s).

You can tweak your keyword list occasionally as you learn what search terms are most productive.

Google Reader

Take your Alerts one step further by adding them to Google Reader, a free tool that constantly checks your favorite news and blog sites for relevant information that you designate. Google Reader aggregates that information into one convenient place and delivers it to you on a schedule that you determine. It also has a built-in public page to easily share interesting items with your friends and family by sending them links. Or add a customizable clip to your site's sidebar that displays your latest shared items. Google Reader also works on any mobile phone browser.

To add Google Alerts to your Google Reader feed, simply create a Folder in Google Reader and add your Alert Feeds to it. Google Reader is an RSS aggregator for the information from sites that you choose to follow, including blogs. Set up your Google Reader account: http://www.google.com/reader

FriendFeed

Listen to your social media friends, and even friends of friends, by using FriendFeed (http://www.friendfeed.com). It allows you to choose and automatically pull in updates from the services you already use, including YouTube, Twitter and Facebook. You see everyone's updates in real time, in one place – so it's easy to track customer, employee and business associates' comments. Then engage them in conversation, or respond to a need, question or issue.

For Facebook, you can add the FriendFeed Facebook application. This app will put FriendFeed on your Facebook profile and in your mini-feed. You will also be automatically subscribed to your Facebook friends who are already using FriendFeed and your friends on the two services will continue to be kept in sync.

How to handle negative comments

The Internet in general, and social media in particular, has essentially equipped every participant with a megaphone and license to use it liberally. Now everyone has a voice and they don't hesitate to use it.

When negative comments show up (and they will), experts agree that excellent PR and customer service skills can turn lemon into lemonade. Not always, but hopefully most of the time.

Respond when it's warranted:

- When you really did goof up. It happens.
- When the negative commentary just isn't true.
- When it starts to spread.

How to respond:

- Quickly. Even if you don't have a solution right way, don't wait until the responsible person comes back from vacation. Post a comment like, "We hear your frustration (or whatever), and we don't have an answer at this moment, but we really do care, and want to resolve this and make you happy. We can respond with a solution by 3pm (EST). In the meantime, if you'd like to talk with our customer service manager, please email, text or call...."
- Remember that the customer is always right. Even when they aren't. This translates into, "Don't argue with the customer."
- Acknowledge your mistake and apologize authentically.
- If you're correcting a misstatement, use genuine diplomacy. Never make the customer wrong. Just deliver more information; "We understand how you could feel this way, so we want to be sure that you know this, to..."

- If negative comments are on a site you control, don't delete all of them. Visitors understand that not everything is perfect. Some negative comments add to your authenticity and build trust.

- If a negative comment spotlights a real problem, and a solution was implemented that actually helps the business, then post a *thank you* for bringing it up.

- Offer the unhappy customer something of value... a coupon? A free e-book?

- Consider posting a video apology!

- Resolve the situation and post it in response so other visitors see the resolution, too.

Have you ever been a dissatisfied customer and experienced great service in response to your irritation? It's the same online. Build positive relationships and the word will spread in a positive way.

Where to begin your network

By creating a social media network, your marketing message can travel far and wide and attract customers fast. To begin, we'll focus on four key social media platforms that work well together: Facebook, Twitter, LinkedIn and YouTube. Then, we'll show you how to tie it all together to create an integrated suite of tools that keep you plugged in - and make your social marketing as efficient and effective as possible.

Introducing Facebook, Twitter, LinkedIn, and YouTube

At the very least, your company should have a presence on Facebook, Twitter, LinkedIn and YouTube. Your company should also have a blog either freestanding, or a feature of your website. As we've discussed throughout these pages, you must incorporate your keywords in prominent places on each property, including the profile. Headlines, subheads, italics and bold, all serve to increase the importance of the keywords in the eyes of the search engines.

When you set them up properly, each of these social media 'properties' will have a link to your site and links to each other. Basically, your visitors should be able to access all of your online properties from any one of them.

Chapter Fifteen Highlights

- The wonder of social media is that it naturally connects people who have similar interests. You want to reach your friends and your friends' friends.

- *The ultimate goal of an Internet marketing campaign is to create a meaningful message that reaches its target audience and is virally spread to others who are interested in the topic.*

- Build your social media presence and interaction very deliberately.

- Begin by listening. Sign up for Google Alerts, a free service that searches Google's index, including blogs, news, video, groups and the Internet, for keywords that you specify.

- Take your Alerts one step further by adding them to Google Reader, a free tool that constantly checks your favorite news and blog sites for relevant information that you designate.

- Listen to your social media friends, and even friends

of friends, by using FriendFeed.

- When negative comments show up – and they will – experts agree that excellent PR and customer service skills can turn lemon into lemonade.

- Respond to negative comments quickly. If you don't have a solution right way, don't wait until the responsible person comes back from vacation. Post a comment like, "We hear your frustration (or whatever), and we don't have an answer at this moment, but we really do care and want to resolve this and make you happy. We can respond with a solution by 3pm (EST). In the meantime, if you'd like to talk with our customer service manager, please email, text or call...."

- Begin to build your social media network – focus on four key social media platforms that work well together; Facebook, Twitter, LinkedIn and YouTube.

- Then tie it all together to create an integrated suite of tools that keep you plugged in.

- When you set them up properly, each of these social media "properties" will have a link to your site and links to each other. Basically, your visitors should be able to access all of your online properties from any one of them.

Chapter Sixteen

* * *

Facebook for Business

How to create your unique Facebook company page and attract your ideal customers

"Facebook is the world's leading social network. But how do you get the most out of it? To answer this question and more, Mashable has created The Facebook Guide Book, a complete collection of resources to help you master Facebook." – Pete Cashmore, Mashable http://mashable.com/guidebook/facebook/

Check out Facebook's own site tour:

http://www.facebook.com/sitetour/homepage.php

How to create a Facebook company page

It wasn't always so, but now it is simple to set up a company account on Facebook:

1. From your Internet browser, go to:
   http://www.facebook.com/pages/create.php

2. Choose a category for your business. I recommend "brand, product or organization."

3. Enter your name (choose carefully) and click on "Create Official Page."

4. Enter specified account info and click "Sign up Now."

5. On the "Get Started" tab, fill in the requested information. Include a link to your site with engaging, keyword-rich descriptions.

6. Link your Facebook Fan Page to your Twitter account.

Using Facebook

Your Facebook profile is the engine that powers your Facebook momentum. When you set up your account, choose your name very carefully, as it cannot be changed.

Complete the profile information carefully, as this is your "face." Use your keywords and don't scrimp on descriptions. What you provide should be authentic, accurate, and informative. This is your opportunity to build your online credibility within the Facebook community, but without brochure-style language. Do not hype.

Post links to your blog, website, and other social media sites so people can connect easily.

How to get traffic from Facebook

Your network is the lifeblood of your Facebook community. It is the audience with whom you create interest in your expertise, information offerings, products, and business. Go back to your ideal customer profile and think about the things that interest them. On Facebook you want to post information, links, and tips that will catch their attention and give value, solve a problem, or meet a need.

Add interesting content in the form of very short "Updates" regularly to keep your community engaged. Socialize by recognizing others' expertise and draw attention to them with links to their sites. They will reciprocate. Incorporating keywords, write brief posts with news, tips, and helpful information snippets. Add photos and videos of your products, using… *keywords*. Post updates a few times a week, perhaps daily, if it's meaningful and interesting. Always keep the tone of your posts in the culture of social media – offering value, not promotion.

The *Like* button lets a user share your content with friends on Facebook. When a user clicks the Like button on your site, a story appears in the user's friends' News Feed with a link back to your website. This word-of-mouth endorsement is *strong*! Friends, and friends of friends, are now made aware of you. Thousands of people can find your info and it has the potential to go viral.

Facebook News Feed

The Facebook News Feed is a top priority for your business' marketing campaign. Your organization should make it a goal to appear at the top of your networks' individual News Feeds as often as possible.

When anyone in your network engages with your brand (shares a photo, RSVPs to an event, posts an update, etc.) a feed item is placed on their mini feed. Live feeds are unfiltered, visible to every individual in your network, and placed prominently on their Facebook page. It's usually the first thing that every Facebook member scans when they arrive at their Facebook page.

Post meaningful comments on others' updates regularly, in order to keep your networking fresh and engaging. This level of interaction personalizes your company and keeps it top-of-mind.

Facebook Notes and Photos

Facebook says it best: "With Facebook Notes, you can share with your friends through written entries. You can tag your friends in notes and they can leave comments. The Notes application page displays notes recently written by your friends, notes in which your friends have been tagged, and links to your own notes." So you reach your friends and also your friends' friends.

Use these features to post information about your brand – always authentically.

Sam Odo, Facebook's product manager for Photos, shares in his blog: "Ninety-nine percent of people using Facebook have uploaded at least one photo. More than 100 million photos are uploaded every day." Facebook is working to make photo sharing and tagging even easier.

Facebook Photos are a marketer's dream, partly due to the ability to "tag" people in photos.

The power of Tagging

Tagging allows the person who posts a photo to name the individuals in that photo and place a link to the individual's Facebook profile.

Photo tagging is a powerful marketing tool for several reasons:

- When you tag someone in a photo, they get a special notification. People LOVE to see and be seen, so when they get notice that their photo has been posted, they forward it on like wildfire.

- The tagged photo you post has a direct link on the wall of the person tagged. So now it is visible to your network as well as THEIR network. Double exposure – double marketing power!

For business marketing, take photos of business receptions or public events in which your company has participated. (Be sure to charge an employee with the responsibility of collecting names!) Add photos to your page and tag them, driving traffic to your Facebook presence, thus boosting awareness and growing your network.

Facebook Events

Facebook Events is another powerful, free marketing feature. When your business holds an event, either online or offline, you can set up a Facebook Event page, and each Facebook invitee will be sent an invitation. Here again, it's powerful for some of the same reasons that photo tagging is powerful. Your invitee receives the invitation and it is posted on their wall for all of THEIR friends to see. You can potentially reach many more people who may not have otherwise heard about the event.

Companies use events for:

- Employee recognition.
- Product launches.
- Press conferences.
- Company milestone celebrations.
- Getting creative!

The Event page tracks all the RSVPs and displays them for everyone to see. When someone visits the Event page (through the link they receive), they can learn more about the event, your company, and perhaps most importantly, which of their friends have responded with an RSVP to attend – viral marketing and personal endorsements in one easy package.

Facebook Groups

Facebook Groups have been around a long time. They are another way to tap into a niche community where your ideal customer engages online. Search for groups in your niche or create your own group. In groups, you can post discussion topics or questions (always adding value and using keywords), relevant videos, photos and links to news and great resources. Send periodic updates to members – and always make them valuable, interesting, and brief.

More Facebook marketing tools

Give your Facebook network reasons to want to engage with your brand. Send them direct messages. Ask for their opinions. Ask for reviews of your products.

- Facebook Messages – Communicate directly with influencers in your niche – How-Tos from their Help section: http://www.facebook.com/help/?page=938 (You must log in to Facebook to access this page.)

- Facebook Polls – Create a poll to engage your target market and do market research: http://apps.facebook.com/opinionpolls/ (You must log in to Facebook to access this page)

Attract website visitors to your Facebook page

To further build your network, add Facebook's social plugins to any web page, such as your website or blog, in order to connect visitors to your Facebook community. The most powerful is the *Like* button (as a site plugin). When a visitor clicks the Like button on your site, a link to your page is added to their Facebook activity for their entire community to see. I personally get business in this way, when friends of friends click on that link out of curiosity.

Not only that, but visitors who click on your Like button will see all of their Facebook friends who also Like your site. This is a dynamic tool to reinforce your credibility and brand. It's akin to getting a recommendation; the most powerful revenue generator is word-of-mouth.

Chapter Sixteen Highlights

- Facebook is the world's leading social network. It is simple to set up a company account on Facebook.

- Your Facebook profile is the engine that powers your Facebook momentum.

- Your network is the lifeblood of your Facebook community. It is the audience with whom you create interest in your expertise, information offerings, products, and business.

- The Like button lets a user share your content with friends on Facebook. This word-of-mouth endorsement is *strong*!

- The Facebook News Feed is a top priority for your business' marketing campaign.

- Use the notes and photos features to post information about your brand – always authentically.

- Photo tagging is a powerful marketing tool, because people *love* to see and be seen. So when they get notice that their photo has been posted, they forward it on like wildfire.

- Facebook Events is another powerful, free marketing feature.

- Facebook Groups are another way to tap into a community where your ideal customer engages online.

Chapter Seventeen

***

Twitter for Business

How to use Twitter to build your business

Twitter is a free communication tool that allows you to send short (140 character) messages (called tweets) to virtually anyone. You can send a tweet to a group or an individual. You can also reply to others' tweets.

✔**Twitter Training Tip:** *"Twitter is a social network used by millions of people, and thousands more are signing up every day to send short messages to groups of friends. But where's the user manual for Twitter? Where do new Twitter users go to learn about tweeting, retweets, hashtags and customizing your Twitter profile? Where do you go if you want to know all about building a community on Twitter, or using Twitter for business? How can you find advanced tools for using Twitter on your phone or your desktop? To answer all these questions and more, we've assembled The Twitter Guide Book, a complete collection of resources for mastering Twitter. Happy tweeting!"*

– Pete Cashmore, Mashable http://mashable.com/guidebook/twitter/

Why use Twitter for business?

Twitter offers businesses a special guide to get the most out of their service: http://business.twitter.com/twitter101 One of Twitter's key benefits is that it gives you the chance to communicate casually with customers on their terms, creating friendly relationships along the way – tough for corporations to do in most other mediums. As a business, you can use it to quickly share information with people interested in your company, gather real-time market intelligence and feedback, and build relationships with customers, partners and other people who care about your company."

Businesses benefit tremendously from using Twitter's quick-connect functionality. Run a Twitter search for your company and follow up to connect with customers who've tweeted about you.

- Reply with "thanks" to happy customers.
- Respond immediately to unhappy customers who tweeted complaints.
- Customers feel "heard" when you contact them.
- Share tips, offer specials, and provide coupon codes.
- Tweets are a rich source of market research.
- Tweets can be spread virally on search engines garnering brand awareness and increasing followers.
- Tweets work well for Business-to-Business and Business-to-Consumer.
- Follow news in your niche.
- Follow competitors for inside info!

How to use Twitter

If you use Twitter for business, handle it in a business-like way. If you handle it in a personal or casual way, you won't get business results. Tweets are searchable, permanent Internet content, so be sure that you're proud of everything you say!

Sign up for Twitter and start listening

Create your Twitter account free: http://www.twitter.com/

- Choose a username that leverages your niche keywords or promotes your business name. It will show up in searches.

- Customize your profile with care, using your logo, keywords and link to your main site.

- Make your brand image consistent with Facebook and all your social media properties.

- Do not select the "Protect Your Tweets" option.

- Send a mass invitation with your Twitter profile link to your network or email database.

- Use Twitter's search function to find people with similar interests – your ideal customers.

- By linking your Twitter account to your mobile phone number, you can receive and write tweets via text message. Look in the mobile help section of Twitter's "Articles" for setup instructions.

- To include shortened URLs in your tweets, convert a long one using a free service such as Bit.ly http://www.Bit.ly (More on this later.)

Link your cell phone to your Twitter account (http://m.twitter.com/login), so when you're waiting in line or simply taking a break, you can tweet or retweet.

Start your Twitter experience by finding and following other interesting Twitter users. Twitter instructs new users to: "Click the *Find People* tab at the top of your Twitter page. You can find and follow other users in these three ways: (1) browse accounts by subject; (2) import your address book contacts to find out which friends are already on Twitter; (3) search one-by-one for people or groups of interest."

Twitter gives you a homepage and a timeline to view incoming tweets from those whom you follow. Click on links in their tweets to view web pages, photos, videos, blog posts, etc.

Start your own tweets

Your tweets will consist of the message, a shortened URL, perhaps a hash tag (#), and a source reference. It could look like this – an example from Clorox:

Learn how to coexist w/ pets in a clean home from this @WebMD article: http://tinyurl.com/yep2jsc We love our pets but they can make a mess!

Hash tags can be inserted in front of a word (keyword) to make it relevant in a search. The hash tag also makes that word relevant in all Twitter searches.

Tweet regularly. Communicate in a business-like way, offering value, news, solutions, or resources you just found. Tweet about a speech you're listening to, a conference you're attending, a reception, a networking event and so on. Remember to use keywords, since tweets are searched and are permanent Internet content. Try to mention other Twitter users by their Twitter username (preceded by the @ sign), which can start a new conversation.

How to tweet like a pro

Twitter has now surpassed many tools for effectiveness in driving traffic to your site. But, you MUST do it like a pro. Your tweet must be created to be:

- Easily and quickly absorbed.
- Easily "retweeted."

Your tweets convey a lot about you, and in business, you want to create a professional impression. Even if you're tweeting to someone you know, it could be retweeted again and again – to people you don't know. So create a polished impression and gain credibility, respect and followers:

- Include the promise of a benefit at your imbedded link, on which you really deliver.
- Don't disappoint, or you'll be shut out in the future.
- Use intelligent grammar, correct spelling and correct punctuation. Like a good first impression, it can't hurt. But it could hurt if you don't.
- Start each sentence with a capital letter, but don't use all caps (which indicates *shouting*).
- Use exclamation points sparingly, if at all.

For more tips on getting started, see Twitter's own guide:

http://business.twitter.com/

After that, dive in deeper with Twitter's Best Practices Guide: http://business.twitter.com/basics/best-practices

> ✔ **Twitter Tip:** *Tweeting the exact same message more than once is a violation of Twitter's Terms of Service. If you want to repeat the message, rewrite your tweets to switch them up a bit. And if you use a promotional message once, send TEN non-promotional messages. Keep the ratio undeniably social – **give** way more than **promote**. Respond to the posts of your followers and click on their links. You'll likely get reciprocal treatment.*

Retweet

Similar to forwarding an email that you think others might find interesting, you can "retweet." What are the benefits of retweeting?

1. Let others (employees, customers, suppliers, etc.) know that you're genuinely thinking of them.

2. Retweeting good content is a way of staying in touch – top of mind.

3. The original tweeter is notified of every retweet. This builds goodwill, so follow your customers, employees and business associates – and retweet their tweets.

How do you retweet? Add this immediately preceding the original message: "RT@username" This signifies that you are: (1) RT – ReTweeting a message; (2) @ - from; (3) username – the Twitter username of the individual. And because all tweets are limited to 140 characters, if you want your tweets to be retweeted, leave out enough characters to accommodate the retweet portion. The industry norm is 115 characters for the original tweet.

In business, the goal for social media marketers is to post Facebook updates that are heavily commented, Liked and shared, can be tweeted and retweeted, potentially go viral and drive readers to your site. Wow. That's a lot of exposure.

Integrate links with your Bit.ly account

To convert long URLs into shorter, more Twitter-friendly URLs, open a Bit.ly account. Do you want to know how often your Twitter posting has been viewed, clicked on and retweeted? Then integrate your Bit.ly settings into TwitterFeed (http://www.twitterfeed.com), and you'll receive detailed analytics. Use Bit.ly's sidebar to make the conversion more convenient: http://bit.ly/pages/tools

Build your Twitter following

Twitter will go through your Gmail, Yahoo! or AOL email database to find their Twitter accounts. You can then follow their activity and contact them with a request to follow you.

If you don't feel comfortable sharing your database, you can use Twitter's search function to find your customers, employees, vendors and business associates by name. Or use keywords to find individuals with relevant interests.

Use Twitter's "Find People" function. Use directories such as Twellow (http://www.twellow.com), a directory of public Twitter accounts with hundreds of categories and search features to help you find people who matter to you – including your ideal customers. Use WeFollow (http://www.wefollow.com), a directory of Twitter users organized by interests. Find people in your ideal target market. The more people you follow on Twitter, the more followers you'll have, too.

Start up conversations and it could lead to great PR, retweets and possibly new business relationships. Stay away from "auto-follow" systems – tools that promise to build your Twitter following automatically. Just spend a few minutes each day finding your ideal customer, using relevant search terms.

Connect Facebook to Twitter

When you post status updates on Facebook, they can be connected directly to Twitter: http://www.facebook.com/twitter (You must log in to Facebook to access this page). It's very simple. Just click, "Link a page to Twitter" and follow the prompts. You can share everything on Twitter, or only items you choose. When posting photos or videos on Facebook, be sure to include commentary with keywords, which is what will appear on Twitter.

Automate postings with TwitterFeed

If you have more than one Twitter (or Facebook) account, or even if you just want to automate the posting of your single Twitter and Facebook accounts, TwitterFeed can do it. You can setup and sync it with your Facebook and Twitter accounts so that it will automatically post every time you submit a blog post.

Chapter Seventeen Highlights

- Twitter is a free communication tool that allows you to send short (140 character) messages (called tweets) to virtually anyone.

- You can send a tweet to a group or an individual. You can also reply to other's tweets.

- Twitter offers businesses a special guide to get the most out of their service.

- If you use Twitter for business, handle it in a business-like way. If you handle it in a personal or casual way, you won't get business results.

- Tweets are searchable, permanent Internet content, so be sure that you're proud of everything you say!

- Link your cell phone to your Twitter account.

- Start your Twitter experience by finding and following other interesting Twitter users.

- Communicate in a business-like way, offering value, news, solutions or resources you just found. Tweet about a speech you're listening to, a conference you're attending, a reception, a networking event and so on.

- Remember to use keywords, since tweets are searched and are permanent Internet content.

- Similar to forwarding an email that you think others might find interesting, you can "retweet."

- In business, the goal for social media marketers is to post Facebook updates that are heavily commented, Liked and shared; can be tweeted and retweeted, potentially go viral, and drive readers to your site. Wow. That's a lot of exposure.

- Build your Twitter following and connect Twitter to Facebook.

Chapter Eighteen

* * *

LinkedIn for Business

The inside scoop on LinkedIn for business development

LinkedIn declares that it's "the world's largest professional network, with over 70 million members and growing rapidly. LinkedIn connects you to your trusted contacts and helps you exchange knowledge, ideas, and opportunities with a broader network of professionals." They offer a short video for an overview of what LinkedIn is and how it can help you: http://learn.linkedin.com/what-is-linkedin/ They also offer a resource to orient new users: http://learn.linkedin.com/new-users/

LinkedIn's focus on business will benefit you in many ways:

- Search engines love LinkedIn profiles. Your business presence will be recognized for those long tail keywords you use.

- Find experts to help you by using LinkedIn "Answers" and "Groups."

- Stay in touch with people who move or change jobs. LinkedIn is your revolving rolodex.

- LinkedIn connects you with sales leads, potential business associates, even jobs.

LinkedIn Groups

Find like-minded groups within your niche and listen to their discussions. Find a LinkedIn Group here: http://www.linkedin.com/groupsDirectory Niche Groups are rich with knowledgeable professionals and interesting discussions. I learn a lot – and keep learning – by following the discussions I find informative.

When you feel comfortable, post comments that add relevant, meaningful content, using your keywords and a link to your site. Meaningful content might include recent news releases relevant to the discussion topic (that you found by search or Google Alerts), links to deeper resources or even your own blog posts!

I suggest that you also search for groups in your city, so you can meet these individuals at a coffee shop if you strike up an interesting conversation. Identify individuals within these groups who are natural influencers and thought leaders in two ways:

- Who seems to be posting the most meaningful information and stimulating the most intriguing discussions?

- Check LinkedIn's "Top Influencer" board.

Once you've identified the thought leaders, follow their discussions and comment occasionally.

> ✔**LinkedIn Entrepreneurs Tip:** *LinkedIn recognizes that entrepreneurs are an important part of the LinkedIn business community. They offer a special page to give insights and best ways to utilize their tools: http://learn.linkedin.com/entrepreneurs/*

LinkedIn business development

LinkedIn offers a host of ways to help you grow your business through its search and connect capabilities. Find individuals and companies in your niche, and begin conversations. Many times, since LinkedIn members tend to be natural networkers, if there's a potential mutual benefit, they are eager to engage with you to explore it. I've personally met many professionals and entrepreneurs this way. Learn more about LinkedIn business development here: http://learn.linkedin.com/business-development/

LinkedIn Events

Though it's considered by many to be an underutilized tool, LinkedIn Events (http://events.linkedin.com/) can connect you to niche-specific offline events where you can meet people who may be your ideal customers, employees or business partners. Browse by type of event, topic or location. You can also create your own offline or online events and promote them here. Remember, your keywords are an important aspect of LinkedIn Events and will help people find it.

LinkedIn works with Twitter

You can tweet your status updates from LinkedIn to your Twitter followers or automatically post your tweets as your LinkedIn status; or do both. It's a great way to add fresh keyword content to your LinkedIn profile. Get the details here: http://learn.linkedin.com/twitter/

Chapter Eighteen Highlights

- LinkedIn connects you to your trusted contacts and helps you exchange knowledge, ideas, and opportunities with a broader network of professionals.

- Find like-minded groups within your niche and listen to their discussions.

- When you feel comfortable, post comments that add relevant, meaningful content, using your keywords and a link to your site.

- Search for groups in your city, so you can meet these individuals at a coffee shop if you strike up an interesting conversation.

- Identify individuals within LinkedIn Groups who are natural influencers and thought leaders. Follow their discussions.

- LinkedIn recognizes that entrepreneurs are an important part of the LinkedIn business community. They offer a special page to give insights and best ways to utilize their tools.

- LinkedIn Events can connect you to niche-specific offline events where you can meet people who may be your ideal customers or employees or business partners.

- You can tweet your status updates from LinkedIn to your Twitter followers or automatically post your tweets as your LinkedIn status; or do both.

Chapter Nineteen

***

YouTube for Business

Attract your ideal customers with your own YouTube channel

Set up your channel to mirror your brand, image, and topics of interest. Choose a username that leverages your niche, keywords or company name.

Videos posted to YouTube are crawled by search engines and recognized through the effective use of keywords and descriptions. Your videos are directly linked to your YouTube account profile, so viewers can click through and learn more about you, find a direct link to your site, and see other videos you've posted. Your video may appear as a choice for YouTube visitors when they watch videos with similar keywords.

Videos on YouTube can be commented on, tagged and shared – helping you spread your content.

Create your own YouTube channel

Set up your own YouTube channel. It will help establish you as an expert in your field, promote your products, and drive traffic to your site. Since video is so visual, you can showcase product demonstrations and engage with your ideal customers in a more personal way. Make videos that are dynamic and interesting!

If you have a YouTube account, you have the capability to set up a channel. It's assigned to you during setup. Your channel makes YouTube a social network, rather than a simple video database. Channels also:

- Display a description of you and your company.
- Display descriptions of your videos.
- List others' videos that you've chosen as favorites.
- List members who are your friends.
- Offer others the capability to comment on your videos.

In this way, channels create instant communities of people who are interested in similar things by choice or keyword.

Compelling video content

Video content can create a more personal relationship with potential customers and take your business one step closer to converting traffic into sales. Let your visitors see you and your company in action. Try videoing a tour of your office, introducing employees and capturing meetings or product shots. Record a presentation or customer testimonial. Promote events with video as a press release. Video your product in use and also be sure to:

- Display your company name, URL and contact info on every video.

- Use a compelling call-to-action.

- Answer customer service FAQs with videos and imbed them in your site.

- Create How-To videos for pressing problems or often-searched questions.

Watch your competitors' videos and popular videos in your niche. (Popular = thousands, or hundreds of thousands of views). Brainstorm a dozen more ways to use video as a powerful marketing tool.

If you're interested in monetizing your videos, apply for YouTube's Partner Program. Revenue-generating opportunities include:

- "InVideo" ads overlaid on your video and banner ads placed next to your video.

- Sharing revenue from rental of your videos.

- Participating in co-marketing relationships with top brand advertisers.

- Selling your own ads.

Chapter Nineteen Highlights

- Videos posted to YouTube are crawled by search engines and recognized through the effective use of keywords and descriptions.

- Your videos are directly linked to your YouTube account profile so viewers can learn more about you, find a direct link to your site and see other videos you've posted.

- Videos on YouTube can be commented on, tagged, and shared – helping you spread your content.

- Set up your own YouTube channel. It will help establish you as an expert in your field, promote your products, and drive traffic to your site.

- Ideas for compelling videos: Let your visitors see you and your company in action. Try videoing a tour of your office, introducing employees and capturing meetings or product shots. Record a presentation or customer testimonial. Promote events with video as a press release. Video your product in use.

- If you're interested in monetizing your videos, apply for YouTube's Partner Program.

Chapter Twenty

* * *

Social Bookmarking for Business

How social bookmarking helps your business

When you get really great news, articles, posts, or other content from your feeds, you can quickly and easily post them on social bookmarking sites and share them with your network. You can also post articles of your own for others to find and share. Keywords are important here, so that others find your content. When they read it and like it, they can vote to endorse it, and thus increase your content's ranking.

Through the many free social bookmarking tools, you can organize and share a collection of industry-specific and niche-specific content that is highly sought-after by your ideal customer. When your business becomes the *source* of this information, the central hub, you will also become known as an expert in the field. You become the "go-to" place, enhancing your credibility, reputation and increasing your traffic through word-of-mouth.

Build traffic from social bookmarking sites

If your content hits the first page of social bookmarking sites like Digg (http://about.digg.com/), Delicious (http://delicious.com/), Reddit (http://www.reddit.com/help/faq) and StumbleUpon (http://www.stumbleupon.com/productdemo/), you can achieve thousands of visitors to your site.

Every time you post content, make sure it is meaningful and worthy of your ideal customer's time and you will gain a reputation for quality. People will listen to you. They will follow you. Now, add your company's articles, ebooks, and resources to the collection in order to further establish your position as a thought leader in your niche.

Experts agree that in order for your content to get noticed, endorsed, and shared, you must incorporate these tips in to your efforts:

1. Choose a popular topic.

2. Write explosive, engaging headlines (with keywords).

3. Capture the readers' attention in the very first sentence of a short (100 characters) description.

4. Keep their attention by delivering value – a surprise or insightful tip, etc. – in the first sentence of the first paragraph.

5. Deliver high quality information throughout. No junk.

6. Make it easy for others to vote by adding a button at the end of the article.

7. Choose your category carefully.

8. Submit it during a weekday, either at the beginning

or end of the day.

9. Ask for your social networks' votes as soon as you post it. Even 60 votes on Digg.com, within 24 hours, can earn front-page position.

10. Do not use automated submitters. They can get you banned.

11. Do prepare for visitors with related articles they will love and an easy-to-find RSS feed option or opt-in box for your newsletter. This will build your database.

12. Try Digg first, and if it does well, this content on other top sites may also soar. Plus, it can be picked up by bloggers which further increases traffic.

✔*Social Bookmarking Tip:* Want to encourage more activity with social bookmarking? AddThis.com http://www.addthis.com/ – a free tool, helps website publishers and bloggers spread their content across the web by making it easy for visitors to bookmark and share on their favorite social destinations. According to their site, "Over 1.2 million sites use AddThis to share content. AddThis does the heavy lifting for you – optimizing service selection, optimizing service icon sizes, maximizing speed while minimizing space and providing industrial strength analytics."

Another free service, SocialMarker http://www.socialmarker.com, can help you spread your link to 50 of the best social bookmarking sites in under 15 minutes. It also helps you get backlinks, increases your traffic, and helps your link get indexed by Google in a matter of minutes.

WordPress offers a good plugin that simplifies social bookmarking for a WordPress blog. (Plugins are programmed features that can be added to a host platform, such as WordPress, to add custom functionality).

Visit this site for a list of dofollow social bookmarking networks: http://dofollow.info/dofollow-social-bookmarking-networks/

Chapter Twenty Highlights

- When you get really great news, articles, posts, or other content from your feeds, you can quickly and easily post them on social bookmarking sites and share them with your network.

- Through the many free social bookmarking tools, you can organize and share a collection of industry-specific and niche-specific content that is highly sought-after by your ideal customer.

- When your business becomes the *source* of this information, the central hub, you will also become known as an expert in the field. You become the "go-to" place, enhancing your credibility and reputation, and increasing your traffic through word-of-mouth.

- If your content hits the first page of social bookmarking sites like Digg, Delicious, Reddit, and StumbleUpon, you can achieve thousands of visitors to your site.

- Every time you post content, make sure it is meaningful and worthy of your ideal customer's time and you will gain a reputation for quality. People will listen to you. They will follow you.

- A free service, SocialMarker, can help you spread your link to 50 of the best social bookmarking sites in under 15 minutes.

Chapter Twenty-One

* * *

Email Marketing

Email **marketing campaigns - easy, effective, and cheap**

Email marketing campaigns have been around a long time. Typically, it's been standard to invite email subscribers to link to your social media platforms. Increasingly, companies are adding newsletter signup forms to their blogs and social media pages. Your objective is to build your email database to reach more potential customers – *your ideal customers.*

When creating an email marketing campaign, take these aspects into consideration:

1. How well are you integrating email with social media marketing? (Offer feeds instead of newsletters, offer mobile options, etc.).

2. Are subscribers interacting with email messages? (Open rates, click-through rates and number of for-

wards, for instance.)

3. Are you creating viral campaigns? (Ask readers to *forward* something of value – a contest, great content, a coupon or an offer for a freebie.)

4. Do you focus on re-engaging inactive subscribers? (Offer them something free, convey a sense of urgency, etc.)

Email campaigns and social media can be used together to achieve different objectives:

1. *To drive traffic to your social media sites:* Attach something of interest or value to your social media site. Then, in the email itself, include a promise of that benefit, directing them to it with a link to your social media site.

2. *To increase email subscribers:* Place a link on your social media site to sign up for your newsletter. The promise of valuable free information – an ebook, white paper, or report – will greatly enhance the signup rate.

3. *To promote sharing of information:* For readers who have not opted in through social media, include social sharing links to make it easier for them to share your content with others.

Link email with social media

Email (a direct response tool) and social media platforms (social communities) are very different in concept. Email has been a one-way communication, while social media is two-way. However, email tools are now beginning to integrate social media. So, email campaigns are becoming vehicles not only for broadcasting messages, but also for listening.

Email marketing services are exploding with new capabilities. Every day, press releases tout the advances and integration techniques that can be achieved through both existing and brand new services.

Some current tactics for integrating social media into email campaigns include:

- Signing up for your e-mails. They must be easy to find and do.

- Imbedding social sharing links in your newsletter.

- Integrating Facebook's *Like* button into email campaigns.

- Collecting email subscribers from your Facebook wall.

- Using a blog to spotlight content from an email newsletter and invite readers to download the full content from a landing page.

- Conducting a poll on a social media platform and delivering the results via email newsletter.

- Gathering social media profile information on your subscribers in order to segment your database.

- Reformatting email campaigns for delivery on mobile devices.

- Pulling social media posts into email, and monitoring the buzz about your company, competition, and customers.

You'll want to track your success and continually improve the results of your email campaigns. Metrics that help you analyze your outcomes include:

- Bounce rates.
- Delivery rates.
- Click-to-open rates.
- Conversion rates.
- Revenue per emails.
- Retention rates.

Start with one campaign and establish baseline metrics. Then change things to improve subject lines (*must* be intriguing), headlines, content, layout, length, call to action, etc. If you change one thing at a time, it will likely give you more meaningful information about what creates improvement.

The email subject line is *by far* the most important element to get right first. If they don't open it, they can't follow through to take action. Get the subject line right first. Create compelling email subject lines.

Email marketing vendors

Different email marketing vendors offer different capabilities. So, depending on your needs, find one that works for you. And if their press talks about their focus on developing more social media integration capabilities, that's an important consideration for you. Email marketing is developing fast, and you want to align with a progressive provider.

A few top choices include:

- iContact (free trial)
  http://www.icontact.com

- Benchmark (free trial)
  http://www.benchmarkemail.com

- ConstantContact (free trial)
  http://www.constantcontact.com

- MailChimp (offers a free version)
  http://www.mailchimp.com

- Emma (great customer service)
  http://www.myemma.com

View a side-by-side comparison, with feature ratings and price information:

http://email-marketing-service-review.toptenreviews.com/

Send updates to multiple sites by email

Posterous (http://www.posterous.com) gives you the ability to send updates to all your Facebook, Twitter, and blog accounts by email! You can add tags and attach photos, videos, and music – virtually any file type or size. It automatically creates your own website, too – all with one post.

Chapter Twenty-One Highlights

- Your objective is to build your email database to reach more potential customers – your *ideal customers.*

- Email campaigns and social media can be used together to achieve different objectives:

- To drive traffic to your social media sites.

- To increase email subscribers.

- To promote sharing of information.

- Email marketing services are exploding with new capabilities.

- Track your success and continually improve the results of your email campaigns.

- Start with one campaign and establish baseline metrics. Then change things to improve subject lines (MUST be intriguing), headlines, content, layout, length, call to action, etc.

- Different email marketing vendors offer different capabilities. This is developing fast and you want to align with a progressive provider.

Chapter Twenty-Two

***

Mobile for Business

Mobile social marketing and networking. It's the future

According to the Mobile Marketing Association (http://www.mmaglobal.com), "Mobile Marketing is a set of practices that enables organizations to communicate and engage with their audience in an interactive and relevant manner through any mobile device or network."

As consumers become more and more reliant on digital communication, the mobile phone has become the primary means of communication, with mobile phone users outnumbering landline users. About 15% of the world's 350 billion monthly text messages are related to commercial or marketing use.

Mobile marketing campaigns have been showcased on American TV shows such as American Idol, The Apprentice, and the Super Bowl. The objectives are clear and straightforward:

- Increase brand awareness.

- Create a customer opt-in database.
- Drive attendance to events or visits to a store.
- Improve customer loyalty.
- Increase revenues.

The use of mobile for couponing, contests, giveaways, and promotions has been the standard.

Mobile marketing campaigns engage consumers in fresh and creative ways:

- Realtors use it at point-of-sale – on "For Sale" signs.
- TV and cable networks utilize it for consumer polls.
- Companies use text codes for promotions.
- Politicians use it during speeches to solicit volunteers and donations.

Mobile has the capability to drive a viral campaign. For instance, a coupon can be sent, with the message to forward it on to friends, either through Twitter or through a social network "update." Add a way to reward the forwarding of the message via a loyalty program and you have a powerful tool that is relatively inexpensive!

For more ways to mount a mobile marketing or advertising campaign, check out, *"The insider's guide to planning and buying mobile media"* by MobiThinking.com:

http://www.mobithinking.com/best-practices/the-insider-s-guide-planning-and-buying-mobile-media

Mobile social networking

According to Pete Cashmore, Founder of Mashable.com – an excellent and intensely-trafficked blog about social media news: "Mobile social networking speaks for itself: people are now sending constant updates to their friends using services like Twitter, while web-based social networks like Facebook and MySpace can be used from mobile devices. This will lead to a lot more overlap between social networking on the web and in real life: you can upload photos to a web profile the second you take them, or add a new friend to your Facebook network moments after you meet in the real world".

Mobile social networking gives you access to the top social media sites from your mobile device.

Use Twitter (http://m.twitter.com/login) on your mobile device, as we've discussed. It's a convenient way to keep in touch and build relationship.

Sites with mobile applications include Facebook (http://www.facebook.com/mobile/) and MySpace (http://www.myspace.com/myspacemobile), among many others. They give you the ability to:

- Send and receive messages and comments.
- Post updates.
- Browse photo albums.
- Check out profiles.
- Add new friends.
- Read and post blogs.

"Effective campaigns often include a competition, event, or survey requiring a response from the user. Those that also include an element of reward or payback for the user (of course, relevant to the experience) are likely to be even more effective." – Peter Ward, Co-Founder, WAYN.com – "Where Are You Now?"

✔*Mobile Web Access Tip:* *With T9space, you can access and use websites from your mobile device. T9space makes big websites small and fast for mobile phones and devices. Use T9space to message your employees, coworkers, and business associates. View photos, and do everything else you typically do on the Internet, from any phone with a basic browser. It's free:*
http://www.t9space.com

Mobile social networks, tools and applications

Social applications for mobile devices are popping up everywhere, fast. A few of them for business are introduced below.

Create a mobile site or blog

Movylo has everything you need to easily create a mobile site or a blog. Movylo gives you a mix of smart tools and features to create your mobile site—just upload your digital contents and Movylo will do the rest. Movylo will convert, resize and adjust all your contents to fit any mobile phone. http://www.movylo.com

Stream live video from your mobile

Molv lets you stream live videos from your phones to the world. So it's like carrying a ready-to-shoot and broadcast camera in your pocket wherever you go. Share those incredible moments or be an eyewitness. Molv streams your video live as you are shooting it, so you don't have to wait till you finish shooting video. (Check compatible phones on their website.) http://www.molv.com

Text to many

Do you have an audience, members, supporters, or patrons? Do they have cell phones? Start your Broadtexter mobile club now and stay connected: http://www.broadtexter.com

Promote your mobile website

With Zinadoo, keep in touch with your community and use SMS (text message) to promote your mobile website. Then create your own voting, subscription, and text in/text out SMS services: http://www.zinadoo.com

Bring your phone, email, chat and social network contacts together in one place

360 is an Internet service for your mobile, PC, and Mac. It brings your phone, email, chat and social network contacts together in one place. Communicate with your friends, see their status updates, share your photos and favorite places – from your phone, PC or Mac: http://www.360.com

Make cheap calls around the world

Get mig33 and you'll be connected to people around the world. IM (instant message), visit chat rooms, send email, share photos, SMS, and, of course, make cheap calls. Connect with friends on social media all at once: http://www.mig33.com

Social media streams to your mobile device

Wadja is a network with utility – working side by side with Twitter, YouTube, Facebook, Google News, Digg, Foursquare, Amazon, and more – to make your online social life just a bit easier. All you have to do is let them know what interests you – yesterday, today, or tomorrow – and Wadja will work behind the scenes to keep the right updates from your favorite social media services streaming into their proper place, color-coded and ready to read: http://www.wadja.com

Dedicated voice and text feedback numbers

Are you making it easy for customers to tell you what they want, love, or hate about your business? 3jam's dedicated voice and text feedback numbers give you immediate insight that could make or cost you money: http://www.3jam.com

Chapter Twenty-Two Highlights

- Mobile Marketing enables organizations to communicate and engage with their audience in an interactive and relevant manner through any mobile device or network.

- Mobile phone users now outnumber landline users.

- The use of mobile for couponing, contests, giveaways, and promotions has been the standard.

- Mobile has the capability to drive a viral campaign. For instance, a coupon can be sent, with the message to forward it on to friends, either through Twitter or through a social network "update".

- Web-based social networks like Facebook and

MySpace can be used from mobile devices.

- Effective campaigns often include a competition, event or survey requiring a response from the user. Those that also include an element of reward or payback for the user (of course, relevant to the experience) are likely to be even more effective.

- Social applications for mobile devices are popping up everywhere, fast.

Chapter Twenty-Three

* * *

Measure and Track

How to monitor your success and tweak for future growth

Measure and monitor your business 'metrics' to get a clearer picture of trends, successes, and issues that need improvement. Smart business owners use metrics to track campaigns as well as longer-term results. Some of these metrics include:

- Visitors, page views, and time spent on site per day/month.

- Social media network size (fans, followers, etc.).

- Quantity of visitor comments (measure level of engagement).

- Sentiment/quality of comments (measure brand reception/reputation).

- Search engine position.

- Leads generated.

- Conversion rates – new sales.

- Backlinks.

To monitor your home site, Google offers a free tool – and a good starting place – Google Analytics.

Google Analytics

Google explains it best: "Google Analytics (http://www.google.com/analytics/) is a free web analytics tool that is hosted by Google. As a result, the reports and features it offers prove to be powerful, flexible, and intelligent.

With Google Analytics you can track sales, conversions, and measure your site engagement goals against threshold levels that you define. You can trace transactions to campaigns and keywords, get loyalty and latency metrics, and identify your best revenue sources. It shows you how visitors actually find and use your site, so you'll be able to:

- Make informed site structure and content decisions.

- Improve your site to help you make decisions on how to convert more visitors into customers.

- Track the performance of your keywords, banner ads, and other marketing campaigns.

- Track metrics such as revenue, average order value, newsletter sign-ups, page downloads, and e-commerce conversion rates."

SEO analysis

To monitor your site's SEO statistics, join for free and download SEO-BOOK's SEO Toolbar http://www.seobook.com/seo-toolbar for browser access to real-time information on links, competitors, social media, nofollow, rank, keyword, feed reader, and more vital information.

Social media analysis

Monitoring social media is very different from monitoring website performance. Tools tend to focus on delivering information that tracks the level of visitor engagement. Applications that allow companies to monitor conversations on the web are popping up like crazy. They focus on the Who, What, and Where of social media.

Before we get into what they do, it's important to understand what they don't do. They *don't*:

1. Calculate Return on Investment (ROI).
2. Analyze sentiments.
3. Interpret findings.

Effective tools *can* deliver:

1. Competitive intelligence.
2. Customer opinions.
3. PR issues.
4. Trend information.
5. Identification of key influencers.
6. Market knowledge.

Helpful social media metrics

Social media metrics can be intricate and involved. Unless such detail is necessary for your business, a few initial metrics can offer a great deal of insight.

Activity:

- Number of posts.
- Frequency of updates.

Engagement:

- Number of followers.
- Number of views.
- Number and content of comments.

Results:

- Number of leads.
- Number of sales.

Social media monitoring tools

Social media monitoring is in its early stages. A wide variety of tools seem to focus on specific aspects of social media. A few tools attempt to gather information from across many different types of platforms. But no one tool, at this writing, offers users a comprehensive dash-board-style overview of all social media activity. More sophisticated tools are either very new or in development, are primarily for large companies (enterprise-grade), and are quite expensive. The following tools offer great information and are all free – or have free versions:

Facebook page analysis

Detailed analysis of the performance of your Facebook business page can be sent to "Admins" weekly by email. Information includes number of fans added, comments, likes, and visits in the past week. Facebook's "Post Insights" feature lets you see the number of impressions and feedback for each post, as well as details about your demographics, longer-term growth, and engagement trends.

More tool choices

Depending upon your business and the kind of information you're interested in tracking, a variety of tools are available to deliver information in real time. Many of them are introduced below.

Post updates to multiple sites at once

Do you want the ability to make one post and send it out to all of your social media platforms?

Ping.fm (http://www.ping.fm) offers you a quick and easy way to post updates to multiple locations at once. It will even monitor an RSS feed and post it to your Ping.fm network as it updates. Ping.fm's dashboard is the command center. After you set up your accounts, you choose those you want to update.

Find brand content across social media platforms

Enter a company name or URL into the Addict-o-matic search bar, and this tool scours the web for timely posts across many favorite platforms, including Flickr, YouTube, Digg, Google Blogs, Truveo, FriendFeed, and many more: http://www.addictomatic.com

Track and monitor 100+ social media properties

With Social Mention, you can track and measure what people are saying about you, your company, a new product, or any topic – across the web's social media landscape, in real-time. Social Mention monitors 100+ social media properties directly, including: Twitter, Facebook, FriendFeed, You-Tube, Digg, Google, etc. http://www.socialmention.com

Search message boards and forums

Boardreader uses proprietary software that allows users to search multiple message boards and forums. Message boards are known as the 'Invisible Web' and pose many problems to traditional search engine spiders because the content is usually very deep and hard to search. In addition, many of these sites change their locations, servers or URLs frequently, presenting special search challenges. Board-reader users can find answers from others who share similar interests. http://www.boardreader.com

Search blogs and track activity

BlogPulse is a search engine for blogs and an automated trend discovery system for blogs. It offers a set of 'Buzz-Tracking' tools that are applied to blog content daily, to track blog activity on key issues, people, news stories, news sources, bloggers and more. http://www.blogpulse.com

Link your blog to Twitter

Set up TwitterFeed to link your blog (or any RSS feed) to your Twitter account. When you update your blog, a tweet is automatically sent out. http://www.twitterfeed.com

Monitor Twitter activity in one place

Want to see everything that's happening on Twitter on your desktop? TweetDeck shows you a live feed, everyone who has tweeted about you, and all the messages you receive. http://www.tweetdeck.com

Schedule tweets in advance

If you want to take time off and know that your tweets will be sent on schedule, use HootSuite, which also integrates with Ping.fm. http://www.hootsuite.com

Send new Twitter followers an automatic welcome

Social Oomph also schedules tweets for later, but an added feature is its ability to help you start to build relationship with new followers by automatically sending them a welcome message. Sweet. Try it here: https://www.socialoomph.com/

Niche Social Networks for your specific industry

Many industry-specific social networks are emerging to serve people with similar interests or businesses. For example, Yelp (http://www.yelp.com) focuses on the bar and restaurant niche, TravelAdvisor (http://www.traveladvisor.com) for the travel industry, and WiseBread (http://www.wisebread.com) for finance. To find a social networking site in your niche, log on to a group or forum in your niche and ask! To find a niche forum, search Google for "(topic) forum".

Chapter Twenty-Three Highlights

- Measure and monitor your business "metrics" to get a clearer picture of trends, successes, and issues that need improvement.

- Smart business owners use metrics to track campaigns as well as longer-term results.

- Google Analytics is a free web analytics tool that is hosted by Google. As a result, the reports and features it offers prove to be powerful, flexible, and intelligent. They show you how visitors actually find and use your site.

- Track metrics such as revenue, average order value, newsletter sign-ups, page downloads, and e-commerce conversion rates.

- Monitoring social media is very different than monitoring website performance. Tools tend to focus on delivering information that tracks the level of engagement of your visitors.

- A few tools attempt to gather information from across many different types of platforms. But no one tool, at this writing, offers users a comprehensive dashboard-style overview of all social media activity.

- Depending upon your business and the kind of information you're interested in tracking, a variety of tools are available to deliver information in real time.

Chapter Twenty-Four

* * *

Your Social Media Schedule

Daily steps to begin

It can be a bit overwhelming to do all these things and run a business, take care of your everyday responsibilities, and engage in your home life. Online business promotion and social media promotion can be distilled down to a schedule that you can execute in a block of time each day.

Schedule time, preferably first thing in the morning, to log on and take care of it. The following list is a general recommendation. You may wish to customize it to your own business goals and preferences. When you have some experience under your belt, step back and revamp your social media engagement plan to optimize the things that give you the best results.

Daily steps

1. Listen to at least three influencers in your niche. Reply or retweet to those that interest you. Even just "Thank you" is valuable.

2. Respond to comments (of your choosing) on your Facebook wall.

3. Post a status update to your social media sites if you have something interesting or of value to share.

4. Post two items of value – a blog entry, an article, group or forum comments, status updates, etc.

5. Visit your blog and read each of your visitors' comments. Acknowledge each of them with a thank you or meaningful comment on the topic. These are important relationship-building touch points.

6. Search and find at least four people to add to one (or more) of your social networks.

7. Be on the lookout for one person on LinkedIn for whom you could provide one professional "recommendation" every week.

8. Be on the lookout for something of value to tweet about.

9. Think about other tasks that may not be daily, but are important:

   • How long has it been since you posted a new video?

   • A new audio?

   • Distributed a newsletter?

   • How many niche sites have you discovered? Are you engaging?

   • How long has it been since you checked your metrics or stats?

Building your community is an ongoing effort. Consistency wins the prize. So take this guide and make it work for you!

Contact Me

I welcome comments, updates, suggestions, constructive criticism, and reader reviews and endorsements. When you contact me, I may not be able to respond to everyone, depending upon the volume, but I will read every message I get.

Email me:

Feedback@TheWebPoweredEntrepreneur.com

To your online business success,

Lisa Chapman

Resources

How to Make Sure the Search Engines Find You

Since Google dominates the search engine market with a whopping 66%+ of all search engine activity (with 16% Yahoo! and 13% Bing - at this writing), these resources focus on how to optimize your results for Google:

How Google finds your site
(Very important to understand)

"Curious about how Google works? Watch a video about how Google finds your site."

http://www.youtube.com/watch?v=Gl3fyqJ6whY&feature=PlayList&p=8F37FE1AB0B7FC3E&index=9

How Google determines search results
(Also important to understand)

"The software behind our search technology conducts a series of simultaneous calculations requiring only a fraction of a second. Traditional search engines rely heavily on how often a word appears on a web page. We use more than 200 signals, including our patented PageRank™ algorithm, to examine the entire link structure of the web and determine which pages are most important. We then conduct hypertext-matching analysis to determine which pages are relevant to the specific search being conducted. By combining overall importance and query-specific relevance, we're able to put the most relevant and reliable results first."

http://www.google.com/corporate/tech.html

Add your website to Google's crawler
(Be sure you're included)

"We add and update new sites to our index each time we crawl the web, and we invite you to submit your URL here."

http://www.google.com/addurl

Google Sitemap Generator
(Get better coverage in search engines)

"Sitemaps are an easy way for webmasters to inform search engines about pages on their sites that are available for crawling. By creating and submitting Sitemaps to search engines, you are more likely to get better freshness and coverage in search engines. Google Sitemap Generator is a tool installed on your web server to generate the Sitemaps automatically. Unlike many other third party Sitemap generation tools, Google Sitemap Generator takes a different approach: it will monitor your web server traffic, and detect updates to your website automatically." – Google Site Map Generator

http://code.google.com/p/googlesitemapgenerator/

Google Sitemap Submitter
(Make sure Google knows about your site)

"Sitemaps are a way to tell Google about pages on your site we might not otherwise discover. In its simplest terms, a XML Sitemap – usually called Sitemap, with a capital S – is a list of the pages on your website. Creating and submitting a Sitemap helps make sure that Google knows about all the pages on your site, including URLs that may not be discoverable by Google's normal crawling process."

http://www.google.com/support/webmasters/bin/answer.py?answer=40318

How to improve your site's Google rankings (Work your way to page one)

"In general, webmasters can improve the rank of their sites by increasing the number of high-quality sites that link to their pages. For more information about improving your site's visibility in the Google search results, we recommend reviewing our webmaster guidelines. They outline core concepts for maintaining a Google-friendly website."

http://www.google.com/support/webmasters/bin/answer.py?answer=35769

Google Webmaster Tools (How visible is your site to Google?)

"Improve your site's visibility in Google search results. It's free. Google Webmaster Tools provides you with detailed reports about your pages' visibility on Google. To get started, simply add and verify your site and you'll start to see information right away."

https://www.google.com/webmasters/tools/sitestatus

How to Increase Traffic to Your Site

Web traffic and SEO – Free tools

http://www.webconfs.com for examining web traffic and search engine optimization.

Google Search Engine Optimization

Official get-started guide

Check out Google's Search Engine Optimization Starter Guide - PDF link on this page.

http://www.google.com/support/webmasters/bin/answer.py?hl=en&answer=35291

Google WebMaster Central
Enhance and increase traffic to your site

"Improve traffic with Google Webmaster Tools. Welcome to your one-stop shop for webmaster resources that will help with your crawling and indexing questions, introduce you to offerings that can enhance and increase traffic to your site, and connect you with your visitors."

http://www.google.com/webmasters/

Google Web Traffic Analytics
See and analyze your traffic data free!

"Google Analytics is the enterprise-class web analytics solution that gives you rich insights into your website traffic and marketing effectiveness. Powerful, flexible, and easy-to-use features now let you see and analyze your traffic data in an entirely new way. With Google Analytics, you're more prepared to write better-targeted ads, strengthen your marketing initiatives, and create higher converting websites."

http://www.google.com/analytics/

Google Website Optimizer
Free website testing

"Website Optimizer, Google's free website testing and optimization tool, allows you to increase the value of your existing websites and traffic without spending a cent. Using Website Optimizer to test and optimize site content and design, you can quickly, and easily increase

revenue and ROI whether you're new to marketing or an expert."
http://services.google.com/websiteoptimizer

Google Trends
Find out what's hot

"With Google Trends, you can compare the world's interest in your favorite topics. Enter up to five topics and see how often they've been searched on Google over time. Google Trends also shows how frequently your topics have appeared in Google News stories, and in which geographic regions people have searched for them most."
http://www.google.com/trends

How to Advertise for Traffic

Advertise Your Business on Google
Pay-per-click advertising page

"No matter what your budget, you can display your ads on Google and our advertising network. Pay only if people click your ads."
https://adwords.google.com

Google AdWords Guide
Learn all the basics

"In this guide, you'll learn all the AdWords basics, including how to begin, what to expect, and how to make the most of your advertising efforts. Click a topic below to get started."
http://adwords.google.com/support/aw/bin/staticpy?hl=en&guide=21899&page=guide.cs

Google DoubleClick for Publishers
Free tool to manage your advertising campaigns

"Google DoubleClick for Publishers (DFP) Small Business is a free hosted ad serving solution that helps you manage your growing online advertising business."
http://www.google.com/intl/en_US/dfp/info/welcome.html

Dig Deeper Into Google's Offerings

Google Groups
Connect with others to get answers

Join a topic-specific group (for example, 'Business') to connect with others, ask questions & learn. http://groups.google.com/

Google WebMaster Guidelines
Find out what the professionals know

http://www.google.com/support/webmasters/bin/answer.py?answer=35769

Google's own Site Map
List of everything Google offers

If you're looking for anything else on Google, you can check Google's own site map: http://www.google.com/sitemap.html

Free Tools to Help You Find Profitable Niches

Shopping.com top searches
What do consumers want?

"The Shopping.com Consumer Demand Index (CDI) makes it easy for you to put your finger on the pulse of consumer demand. With millions of shopping searches conducted each week, the CDI reveals emerging trends and hidden gems while highlighting the hottest products. View the top 100 searches for each of the Shopping.com categories. These searches are updated every two weeks." – Shopping.com

http://www2.shopping.com/top_searches

AOL hot searches
What's most searched?

"Visit AOL – Search for current hot topics and today's most searched news and keywords." – AOL

http://hot.aol.com/

Delicious Popular
Hot topics today

"Most popular bookmarks. Do you ever wonder what's hot right now on the Web? Or are you looking for the most popular Websites on a specific topic? Delicious is the answer. The Delicious home page shows you the hottest bookmarks on Delicious right now. You can also explore what's hot for any particular topic by checking out the most popular bookmarks for any tag." – Delicious

http://del.icio.us/popular

Digg
Interesting and unique content

"Digg is all about sharing and discovery. There's a conversation that happens around the content. We're here to promote that conversation and provide tools for our community to discuss the topics that they're passionate about. By looking at information through the lens of the collective community on Digg, you'll always find something interesting and unique." – Digg http://www.digg.com/

Technorati
Search blogs for content

"Technorati is an Internet search engine for searching blogs." – Wikipedia
"Technorati Authority measures a site's standing & influence in the blogosphere." – Technorati http://www.technorati.com/

Craigslist
Free classifieds

"Craigslist is a centralized network of online communities, featuring free online classified advertisements – with sections devoted to jobs, housing, personals, for sale, services, community, gigs, résumés, and discussion forums." – Wikipedia
http://www.craigslist.org/

More Resources to Help You
Master and Automate Your Business

The Facebook Guide Book
How to get the most out of Facebook

"Facebook is the world's leading social network… But how do you get the most out of it? To answer this question and more, Mashable has created The Facebook Guide Book, a complete collection of resources to help you master Facebook." - Pete Cashmore, Mashable
http://mashable.com/guidebook/facebook/

The Twitter Guide Book
Complete collection to learn how Twitter works

"Twitter is a social network used by millions of people, and thousands more are signing up every day to send short messages to groups of friends. But where's the user manual for Twitter? Where do new Twitter users go to learn about tweeting, retweets, hashtags and customizing your Twitter profile? Where do you go if you want to know all about building a community on Twitter, or using Twitter for business? How can you find advanced tools for using Twitter on your phone or your desktop? To answer all these questions and more, we've assembled The Twitter Guide Book, a complete collection of resources for mastering Twitter. Happy tweeting!" – Pete Cashmore, Mashable http://mashable.com/guidebook/twitter/

Updates

To find updates and helpful new tools that may not have been available that the time of publication, I publish a companion website for additional resources. A complete downloadable list of links is also available: http://www.TheWebPoweredEntrepreneur.com